2012
Creating Your Own Shift

Shift Awareness Books
For A Better Perspective

2012: Creating Your Own Shift

Cover Artwork by Amoraea Dreamseed

Editing and design by Adonna, with editing assistance from Hunt Henion

ISBN 978-0-9822054-6-4
Library of Congress Control Number: 2011921309

Printed in the United States of America
Shift Awareness Books
www.ShiftAwareness.com

Contributors and Authors

Adele Ryan McDowell, Ph.D.
Adonna
Adolphina Shephard
Amoraea Dreamseed
Anrita Melchizedek
Barbara Joye
Barbara Schiffman
Brie Liberty
Camille Leon
Cat Thompson
C. Norman Shealy, M.D. Ph.D.
Colin Whitby
Cynthia Sue Larson
Dawn Newton
Dolores Cannon
Drunvalo Melchizedek
E. Dee Conrad
Elizabeth J. Foley
Hunt Henion
Justin Wilkinson
Linda Martella-Whitsett
Dr. Linda R. Backman
Marion Ross, Ph.D.
Martine Vallée
Mike Quinsey
Dr. Nina Meyerhof
Patricia Webb
Paul Von Ward
Perry
Rev. Rhonda Smith, Ph.D., D.D.
Sheldan Nidle
Steve Bhaerman
Suzanne Lie, Ph.D.
Suzanne Ward
Sylvia Bucek
Tracy Latz, M.D., M.S., Mh.D
Wendell Fitzgerald

Description for the
"Divine Human Blueprint" cover art

by Amoraea

Upon the throne or ritual platform of the earthly kingdom stands a woman, woven into the precious fabric of Nature with all Her glorious elements. Arising to the status of Priestess, taking sovereign ownership of her own seamless connection to God, and penetrating through the mysteries of the veils between dimensions, she stands at the Gateway where all dimensions of her being converge.

She now opens and ascends to her Higher Self Image or soul body (though in truth her Soul created the image of her fleshly incarnation in the hierarchy of becoming). This is the pinnacle of her being in form, the subtle ether of the Soul Body, and once established there, the bridge is now connected to rise beyond the form into the superluminal formless essence of pure Being.

Our Soul Star is situated like a precious pearl within the Cosmic Source, united with the radiant omniscient Matrix of Intelligence and genesis medium that unceasingly pours forth creationary blueprints. The Human Blueprint is a Sacred Covenant between Source and our Soul to reflect Its Light all the way into the third dimension and awaken as embodied consciousness, capable of expressing and realizing Itself as Source.

(Visit Amoraea's website to view more of his visionary art at www.Divine-Blueprint.com)

Contents

Restructuring Our World

Visions of the Future

Introduction

By Hunt Henion

2012: Creating Your Own Shift summarizes the best insights thirty-seven of the world's most authoritative sources have to offer, providing readers with a vast cross-section of information and perspectives.

One of the most respected and well-published contributors to this anthology states unequivocally:

> *"None of the dire situations that some analysts and some channeled messages purport to be likely, or even unavoidable, will come to pass."*

Others describe dire-sounding situations that may be necessary for our world's renewal. Still other equally respected authors suggest our space brothers will continue to protect us from the most dire of possible situations.

One thing on which all the authors of this work agree is that **2012 will mark an initiation into a completely new consciousness and a divinely ordained new beginning for our world.**

Some discuss how to prepare for this on an individual level. Others suggest needed institutional reforms. Topics discussed range from the esoteric to the down-to-earth.

Authors have condensed the body of their works into concise summaries, exposing readers to the essence of their unique knowledge and discoveries; many also end their sections with information on how readers can access additional details.

This prophetic anthology explains what's happening in our world and what "ascension" is all about. It recommends ways to cooperate with the changes on personal and social levels. The book ends with inspirational visions of the future, mapping the way to a harmonious new world with more humanitarian priorities.

Transition & Transformation

"We are here to re-grow the Garden, and have a heaven of a time doing it." — Swami Beyondananda

Ascension and Spontaneous Evolution

by Steve Bhaerman

As the date "2012" looms closer and closer, there seems to be a quickening. Every planetary crisis — ecological, economical, political and spiritual — is intensifying. There is a sense of impending apocalypse. The scientists are pointing to what they are calling the 6th great extinction. Evangelicals are speaking about the "end times" and a rapture that will sweep them into the sky and leave their clothing for the rest of us. Others are buzzing about changes that will be ushered in by 2012. In other words, everyone knows there is something unprecedented going on.

However to truly understand these times, we must consider the original meaning of the word "apocalypse."

"Apocalypse" means "the lifting of the veils."

Indeed, the veils are now being lifted on political horrors and economic exploitation that many of us have been unwilling to look at. A new book called *JFK and the Unspeakable: Why He Died and Why It Matters*, by Christian theologian Jim Douglass, offers compelling evidence that John Kennedy's assassination was orchestrated by America's military industrial complex. Another noted theologian, David Ray Griffin, has poked holes in the official 9/11 story through *The New Pearl Harbor*, and several subsequent books. Wikileaks has revealed the evil-doings of the American empire, and appears to have just scratched the surface.

The good news is, along with the awful truth comes the awesome opportunity. The veils are also being lifted on ancient spiritual practices kept in "protective custody" for millennia, so that now any individual with the desire and focus can learn shamanic healing, chi kung and the secrets of the Kabala. In other words, the veils are being lifted to reveal our true power, our true destiny so that we can "overgrow" a system of domination that has "outlived its uselessness."

All around us, we see institutions that once served society — the health care, economic, education systems, for example — devolving into dysfunction. Combine this with accelerating environmental and political crises, and we seem to be facing a mega-crisis that cannot be solved by more of the same. It would seem that some kind of miraculous healing is required.

It turns out that we actually have a template for miraculous healing. It's called "spontaneous remission." Every day individuals are told they are terminally ill, and that there is nothing more that medicine can do for them. And a certain percentage of these folks — you may know one, or you may *be* one — miraculously recover. One day the disease is there, and the old test results show it, and the next day it is not — and the test results show that, too.

We can simply ascribe this spontaneous healing to amazing grace or a Divine intervention or simply an unexplainable fluke of nature. However, there may be something more tangible at work. In his study of numerous patients who underwent spontaneous healing, Dr. Lewis Mehl-Madrona (*Coyote Medicine*) found that these healings were often preceded by a "change of story."

This is right in line with the work of cellular biologist Bruce Lipton (*The Biology of Belief*), who shows — from a biological standpoint — how our beliefs and perceptions determine our reality. Bruce and I have co-written another book, *Spontaneous Evolution: Our Positive Future and a Way to Get There From Here*, which applies his breakthrough ideas to our collective beliefs. In other words, it could very well be that the key to planetary healing and transformation is a change in our collective story.

Perhaps the changes we can anticipate around 2012 involve a critical mass of the heretofore-uncritical masses releasing the old story of dominate-or-be-dominated in a "me vs. you" world, and embrace the new story that takes evolution one step further. Every phase of evolution, from the first single cell organisms combining into multi-cell ones, to the development of complex 50-trillion cell communities like our own bodies, has involved two things: expanded awareness, and increased community. This increase in connection and consciousness would indicate that the next phase of human evolution is recognizing that we are each and all cells in a new super-organism called Humanity.

If we look at our human collective consciousness right now, we might conclude that a better name for our species would be Inhumanity. By default — and through fear, manipulation, and programmed beliefs we have until now accepted as "reality" — we have allowed the worst of our so-called "human nature" to rule the world. However, this rule by the "lowest common dominator" is no longer workable. The survival — and *thrival* — of Humanity depends on our willingness and ability to "think like a species."

And more and more, research shows that "thinking like a species" begins with "thinking from the heart." The Beatles said, "All you need is love," and now science is proving them right. Thanks to the work of Dr. Leonard Laskow (*Healing With Love*), and the HeartMath Institute, we now know that positive, loving intention can shrink cancer cells in a Petri dish, and that human hearts entrain with one another like vibrating tuning forks. We've seen experiments where a threshold number of Transcendental Meditators measurably reduced the crime rate in Washington, D.C. A gifted healer, Mahendra Krivedi, has likewise directed the power of Universal Love to heal disease in plants, animals and humans.

Could it be that what we call "ascension" is really the application of this mysterious loving force in our daily lives? Is 2012 the time when this power of love and coherence is publicly acknowledged, and we spontaneously evolve from struggling individual cells into a sane and healthy Humanity? Is our spontaneous remission really a spontaneous "re-missioning" — to live our love fully in the context of connection with not just other humans, but all our relations?

We seem to be right on the cusp of this spontaneous healing and emergent change. What is required is the "practice" of evolution — expanding our individual awareness, and linking up with others willing to gather under "one big intent": To re-grow the Garden and have a heaven of a time doing it.

Will we achieve this evolutionary transformation? Join the "up-wising" and stay attuned …

(Steve Bhaerman is an internationally-known author, comedian and political visionary who has spent the past 25 years writing and performing as Swami Beyondananda, the "cosmic comic." On the serious side, he is the author with Bruce Lipton of *Spontaneous Evolution: Our Positive Future and a Way to Get There From Here* (Hay House, 2009). He is also active in transpartisan politics, and can be found online at http://www.wakeuplaughing.com.)

"It is so important to remember — especially at times of great dramatic impact — that your safety lies within, that no solution that matters in the long run of things will be found outside of yourself. Your answers lie within. ... Trust your feelings." — *The Hosts of Heaven, shared by Adonna*

A Time of Great Change

by Adonna

The late Terence McKenna's greatest legacy to us was his discovery of the fractal nature of time. He and his associates were able to distill this into the mathematics that could trace events within time as a wave that oscillated between periods of "habit" and periods of "novelty." The mathematics were put into a computer program that came to be called Timewave Zero. Graphs generated by the computer program show regular oscillations between times of habit (business as usual) and times of novelty (changes in habit). It doesn't seem to matter what period of time is looked at. The fractal nature of time is still present and revealed as oscillations between habit and novelty. However, in the graph for 2010, a dramatic tipping point was indicated to occur around November 14 and last through January 18, 2011.

This tipping point marked the beginning of an interval that is shaped differently than the rest of the timewave that precedes and follows it. It is smooth and has a constant slope of around 45 degrees downward from a point of maximum habit to a point of maximum novelty that is only surpassed at the end of the timewave itself, sometime near the end of 2012. This seems to imply a constant degree of movement through time toward more and more change or — put another way — that change is building upon change.

The timewave for our present reality reveals a point of maximum novelty that occurs toward the end of 2012. However, due to the fractal nature of time, the closer we get to the end of that wave, the more we experience a "revisiting" of prior historical periods, such that the rate of the cycles of change appears to become faster and faster. Following the tipping point, the amplitude of the oscillations between habit and novelty gradually decreases, so that what we can expect is an overall trend of increasing change and less of a return to the habits of the past. McKenna felt that at the end of the timewave, there would be an explosion into an infinite potential for novelty, and he was at a loss to describe what would happen after that.

This phenomenon of increasing rapidity of change in the cycles of human experience had also been observed by the late Ian Xel Lungold. Lungold adopted an interpretation of the Mayan Long Count that shows that the same amount of change occurs over shorter and shorter periods of time as we move forward and upward through the various divisions and levels of the count. He felt that the Mayan count traced movements into increasingly higher levels of consciousness. In Lungold's model, each succeeding level upward encompassed the same amount of change as had occurred in the level beneath it, but in 1/20th of the amount of time. Both McKenna and Lungold expected a major shift in both the consciousness and the intensity of the human experience, and both were describing a fractal relationship to time, but measuring and describing it slightly differently.

Fractals are also mentioned in the Messages that make up the foundational information for *Operation Terra*, and which were telepathically transmitted by a group of beings who refer to themselves as the Hosts of Heaven. They speak of fractals and iterations, decision points, and logic branches as part of the way the manifest portion of reality operates. The Hosts have also told us that we are approaching the end of an entire cycle of Creation, after which an entirely new Creation will come forth. Their "long count" spans approximately 4.5 billion years, the length of a Day of Brahma in the ancient Vedic system.

Regardless of which system you use, or how you choose to interpret its implications, one thing becomes quite clear: we have reached a point in the overall process in which the amount of change is going to accelerate tremendously and most of us are going to experience these changes while we are still in our physical bodies.

Because of the repetitiveness of the cycles implied and contained in a fractal, experiences and information from the past is also relevant to the present and future, as we experience them within linear time. This is also true of the content of the Messages, parts of which are even more relevant to us today than they were when they were first received and communicated. On August 18, 2002, the Hosts had this advice to offer:

"We cannot emphasize too much that it is important to remain detached and to not get caught up in the drama that is unfolding all around you. The moment you engage with chaos, you get sucked into it. The moment you polarize to something you observe, you get locked into that which you polarize to. It is so important to remember — especially at times of great dramatic impact — that your safety lies within, that no solution that matters in the long run of things will be found outside of yourself. Your answers lie within. Even if you are not hearing "voices" or words, you do know — in each and every moment — what is true for you. You can access this knowing at any time. It is a feeling that you feel. Something will feel "right" or it will feel "off" or "wrong." Trust your feelings. Don't let anyone talk you out of them.

It is not important that anyone else know what you feel. It is perfectly all right to keep your knowing to yourself, but don't let anyone sway you. There will be many attempts to talk you into adopting a certain attitude, but stay aligned with what you know as your own truth. You can carry it silently, but do not abandon it in order to accommodate anyone else."

"… A moment is a unit of experience. It has a beginning, a middle, and an end. You can feel when something begins to rise in energy in your life. It presents, then it swells to a climax, and then it recedes and resolves. That is a moment — from the time it arrives into your life until it recedes and resolves. Every moment arrives containing everything it needs for its completion. It unfolds perfectly, and even when you are in the midst of a challenging time, you can remain rooted in the moment and thus move through it with Grace. The more you can detach — the more you can ALLOW THE MOVEMENT — the more ease and comfort you will have in your journey through the days ahead. Resistance of any kind blocks the flow. You can remain rooted in your truth without resisting the flow that occurs all around you. Think of a tree with a stream flowing around it. The tree remains in place when it is rooted and grounded. Be that tree. This is not the same as stubbornness or resistance. Be rooted in the moment. Be rooted in your truth.

Keep your "inner ear" turned on and listening at all times. It helps to trust the flow of your life. If you feel overwhelmed by the speed of everything, just let it flow. Become still in the midst of the movement that is going on all around you. Let it flow. You are a great being, experiencing yourself as a little body. You are a great being who has helped create vast portions of the existing reality. Breathe. Center. Ground. Bring calm to yourself as a choice. Choose calm. Choose peace. Choose serenity."

Good advice for navigating the tremendous changes just ahead and beyond! I wish you a good journey, and hope that what is written here helps to make it an easier one for you.

Sincerely,
Adonna
November 10, 2010

(Adonna is the custodian of and spokesperson for the material related to Operation Terra. You can read all of the available material at no charge at www.operationterra.com. It is also available for purchase as printed books anywhere in the world. Adonna can be reached at adonna@operationterra. com. This article is copyrighted and may be distributed without modification if proper credit is given and the web site and e-mail address are included.)

"Basically, the shift of the ages involves a shift in the vibratory rate of the world. … Currently we are all going through a quickening process, a speeding up of the frequency at which our very bodies vibrate." — Adolphina Shephard

2012 — The Missing Key

by Adolphina Shephard

There has been much speculation and many prophecies surrounding the mystery of 2012. However, there is something missing in all this wealth of information. Almost all information given surrounding 2012 is about how a scientist, researcher or author has uncovered key facts in order to prove that something really big is going to occur in 2012 — the Precession of the Equinoxes, the Long Count Mayan Calendar — all of this information makes for a fascinating subject to study regarding what is coming on December 21, 2012.

However, more important than knowing that something big is coming in 2012 is to be prepared for the coming "Shift of The Ages." What is lacking is the "Missing Key." The "Missing Key" is what to do and how to do it, in order to prepare yourself for the coming shift, so that you not only survive but thrive!

Knowledge without action is worthless! Yet, what are we really supposed to do about all this? What's our personal key for preparation and putting it all in perspective?

Basically, the shift of the ages involves a shift in the vibratory rate of the world. One key that is missing in most discussions about this is how we can increase our vibrations to stay in synch with Mother Earth, who is ascending. At this point, there's no turning back for those who want to stay in harmony with her. The wheels of this event were initially put in motion millions of years ago.

Currently, we are all going through a quickening process, a speeding up of the frequency at which our bodies vibrate. This involves a quickening from the portal activations that God is faithfully sending out on a regular basis! This is also why many of us are tired a lot of the time. Our bodies are changing. At this time, mankind resonates on a vibration of anywhere from 275-2,800 megahertz. However, where we are headed is going to require a frequency of 6,000 megahertz.

Even with the portal activations that God is sending through on a regular basis, without us doing our homework, the maximum level to which our frequency can be raised is about 4,000 megahertz. Those who are resonating at 2,000 and above will not have much of a challenge. However, those resonating at 275 might feel very challenged.

Raising our vibrations is a requirement for mankind, which could be viewed from the perspective of free will. In others words, God will not force you to ascend with Mother Earth. Those wishing to ascend to a higher dimension must exercise their own efforts to increase their vibratory level. After all, we're talking about progression of the human species to what we would now consider a super human!

What is occurring at this time is that old traumas, karma, and blockages are being forced to the surface through the portal activations from God. This is why you see so many people acting crazy, doing crazy things. Spiritual, emotional and mental traumas are being forced to the surface for release. Most Lightworkers have been removing density from their bodies for years now, in preparation. However, all of us must now do some of the simple things that are outlined in this book to prepare our physical bodies for the coming shift.

This adjustment is necessary in order for our bodies to ascend with the Earth, because our bodies must go from being carbon-based to crystalline-based. In a lot of ways, it is like compressing carbon into a diamond. **Our carbon-based bodies are actually changing into spiritual jewels!**

We must prepare our bodies and minds for this. That's the key to thriving through the ascension process. While most of the world around you swirls in chaos, those who do their spiritual homework will be in the calm center of the storm and will ride the waves of ascension like a dolphin riding the waves of the ocean.

This is the moment of preparation. Time is of the essence. We must prepare ourselves to rise above a third-dimensional reality. "The Light Body" is our physical double. It just vibrates at a higher frequency and is therefore less dense. In ancient times, achieving conscious oneness with your Light body was recognized as the "ultimate" primary goal, said to grant you immortality forever.

Through time, we have simply forgotten how to relate to life from our Light bodies. As the world became more modern and industrialized, we fell away from spiritual practices.

Most religions, cultures or traditions, are aware of the Light body, although different religions or cultures refer to it by different names. In Christianity, it is often referred to as "The Resurrected Body." Buddhism calls it either the "Light body" or the "Rainbow Body." Taoism calls it the "Diamond Body." Sufism calls it "The Most Sacred Body." It is called "The Glory of the

Whole Universe" in alchemical tradition. In Hermaticism, it is known as the "Immortal Body." What all of these religions and traditions have in common is that achieving conscious oneness with your Light body is the ultimate goal. In this way, we are integrated in mind, body and spirit with our yin/yang in perfect balance. Our personal will has aligned with God's Will. For now, we realize we came to be of service and have a mission to fulfill.

One thing that must be understood is that our primary soul or monad is always immortal, but our physical bodies are not, at least not until they reach that vibratory level. And that level will probably be within reach sometime in 2012, when an entirely new cycle begins for humanity.

2 Corinthians 4:17-18: "For our light affliction, which is but for a moment, worketh for us a far more exceeding and eternal weight of glory. We do not rejoice in the things which are seen, but in the things which are not seen; for the things that are seen are temporal, but the things which are not seen are eternal."

In anticipation of the coming shift, doesn't it make sense to simply prepare yourself on all levels of being? Preparing your spiritual, mental, emotional, and physical bodies *energetically* is the "Missing Key" to achieving harmony with your immortal Light Body.

All mankind has the potential to move into harmony with their Light body. Yours may be lying dormant, just waiting for the lifetimes of grimy, dark, dense energy to be cleared away. *This occurs primarily through activations, attunements, and Energy Work or Energy Medicine.*

Much work must be done in a disciplined, consistent manner to remove lifetimes of blockages and traumas, which are stored in your chakras, your Grid System, your Meridian System, your Prana Tube, right down to your cells. All of these blockages must go before the body can heal and prepare for attunement with the Light body. Seek out help with this through Energy Medicine such as Chakra Balancing, Karma Clearing, Grid Repair, etc. either through learning how to do these things yourself or through an established Energy Medicine Pratitioner. To get you started, simply ask, "God, please prepare me for the Shift of The Ages."

Romans 13:12 The night is far spent, the day is at hand. Therefore let us cast off the works of darkness, and let us put on the armor of light."

We are preparing ourselves, the world over, for the birth of The Christ Consciousness. All who choose to be the receptacle for this consciousness will help to build a bridge between Heaven and Earth. This awakening and evolution of mankind is the "Shift Of The Ages" — the birth of the new super human!

It won't matter who wears what clothes or how thin or how fat they are, what car someone drives, or where someone lives. We will know people by their energy, the feeling they exude, and the aura of their Light body. Immediately, you will know a kindred soul when you see them and feel their love, or see them shining with a rainbow of colors.

If there is a high enough percentage of enlightened beings, much of the rest of humanity has the potential to be pulled into their own Light body through a process called *entrainment*. The process of entrainment occurs when electrons move into phase or resonance with each other. The scientific term, "entrainment," was originated by physicist Christian Huygens in 1666, and the concept is similar to the 100th monkey theory that most of us have heard about.

Due to entrainment, it is possible that much/most of mankind may successfully ascend on the back of Mother Earth. This is our highest hope and aspiration. With all the energies being sent to Earth by God to raise the consciousness, frequency and vibration of mankind, we now have the opportunity to become our own savior!

What is also occurring at this time is that the template for a new "Garden of Eden or "Heaven on Earth" is emerging in the planet's Light body. It will be where all of mankind will realize that we are one race, "the human race," and we will have one religion, the religion of "love."

Fear not and prepare for this unprecedented time. Build what you would like to see occur on Earth, such as peace, joy, a roof over everyone's head, and food in every belly. All it takes is a little prep work on our part to attain peace for ourselves and our loved ones.

(Adolphina Shephard is a planetary healer, the Founder of YATUVAY Energy Medicine School, and the author of *YATUVAY ~ The Manual, How To Perform Miraculous Healing*, and *Living With Spirit ~ Going Beyond the Physical*.

See www.AdolphinaShephard.com. To contact Adolphina, e-mail her at AdolphinaShephard@msn.com.)

Our Divine Blueprint

by Amoraea Dreamseed

The Quest for the Soul, for some greater purpose and design to our existence, is written into the fabric of our psyche. Hardwired not only into our psyche, but also in our very biology, is the drive to "spiritualize" matter, to make it a more complete and self-aware expression of the Creator.

Though our soul's great weave spans many more worlds and dimensions than just the experience of planet Earth as a human, it is here in these bodies that a pivotal transformation and anchoring of certain teachings, assimilations, and purpose will occur. For us to get a true sense of what is happening during this massive shift as we travel towards 2012, all must be put into the context of a shamanic or spiritual awakening — "The Hero's Journey," as Joseph Campbell would term it. There must be a death for the new greater Self to emerge.

But the graduation of the self into "Enlightenment" or "spiritual illumination" is not a new reality — awakened masters have blessed cultures throughout the ages, from Christ to Buddha, from the Yogis of India to the Sufis of Persia, and the Taoist Immortals in China … No, the new prospect occurring on the planet now is the globalization of consciousness and the building of our awareness as an entire species into something greater.

There are certain cycles within humanity's evolution where the energetic wave of time propels us to become something more than we have been — not just a maturing of our species, but an actual LEAP into a whole new stage of being. For instance, the birth of Homo sapiens, the rise of agriculture and its impact on our way of life, the birth of civilization around Egypt and Sumeria, the concept of monotheism from pantheistic beliefs … these are huge rings within the growth of our "Tree of Life."

Could we be at the cusp of another leap? Does 2012 herald the dawn of a new species? In the Mayan understanding of time, 2012 was to be the closing and opening point of a huge cycle of Creation, much like what the Vedic Indians believe about the Yuga Cycles, which are connected to the Inbreath and Outbreath of Brahma or Creator. As we are being pulled towards 2012, it is like the great inbreath for our species where everything that we have created is tested against the fire of Brahma's Truth!

Whether for an individual or a whole species, any massive transformation is a very tenuous experience — we're not who we have been anymore, and we are at the cusp of becoming something else we are not quite yet. It is during these times we get a true sense that something beyond our little self is at the "helm of the ship."

From all sides of the new scientific frontiers, we are waking up to the fact that our entire species is much like individual cells that form a larger biological entity (humanity). There is a biological "internet" that links all human beings not only to each other, but to Gaia/Earth as our parent organism.

Could it be that we as a species are actually guided by our future, and that some phenomenon taking place in 2012 is steering the ship of humanity towards a course that has an intelligent goal beyond our individual minds' conception? Quantum physicists and those studying black holes talk about attractor points and event horizons. As we know from Einstein, space and time are not separate but are actually one entity that we call spacetime. In a black hole, even time collapses! Perhaps certain points in time are like black holes with their own kind of gravity, which influences the cycles of time close to it. 2012 may be one of these points that is pulling our consciousness into it, towards a vortex or zero-point where the veils are thinned and we can come in touch more directly with the Source of All Creation. One thing is certain: time appears to be speeding up! Information is becoming accessible faster, technology is advancing exponentially, and in a similar fashion, many people are also waking up rapidly to their higher nature.

Above and beyond any shift happening on the outside, in the world's conditions, is the shift happening within ourselves because of the quickening of energies brought on by our approach to 2012. Many are being jolted awake from the slumber of their "previous" life, which can quickly deconstruct and decay amidst the higher-vibrational force of the Soul anchoring. It's almost as if there is a second reincarnation of the soul into the adult awareness, a process which we weren't cognitive of when we were first born.

I call the Soul's original design our "Divine Blueprint." It is the unchanging deathless part of us that — here in human time — is becoming more and more aware of itself. In a sense we are getting glimpses of our perfect nature and we are letting that perfect awareness (of our Soul) transform our body and our mind to match it. Right now, we are working on opening up our whole being to allow more light to infuse it, transform it, and then pour through it to share with others — to share with the collective body of humanity.

The emphasis on engaging our Divine Blueprint is equally and ALL-ways on both personal and planetary activation. More and more we are recognizing ourselves as a seamless inseparable whole in which all personal evolution is simultaneously done for the collective. We are entering an alliance in which the planet's ascension is firing up through our individual circuits to complete a planet-wide project of awakening. We lift into a higher-dimensional awareness so that our consciousness scopes beyond the personal and yokes into a transpersonal, collective serviceship. Literally, we are building a "ship" in which humanity as a whole can travel to another bandwidth of being!

It may be nothing new. Humanity may just be coming on track to the common evolutionary route that consciousness takes once a species' nervous system and genes reach a certain level of capacity and maturity around its local sun. But for the species involved in this chrysalis process, it is a supremely spectacular event of awakening to its next step within the growth spiral!

All evolution occurs first through those pioneers riding the crest of new consciousness who will set the next Divine Blueprint of the emerging global community. First we must recognize ourselves as those pioneers by acknowledging and acting from our own sovereign power as an "Ambassador of Light." The more our own crystalline luminous body is developed and activated, the more easily we can connect to the planetary grid. We help stabilize the grid together through optimizing our own central axis and sustaining high frequency! We must anchor the potency of our divine presence enough to realize we have the power to manifest, guide, and direct the frequency wave of enlightenment onto the shores of collective humanity. WE set the tone for the next harmonic attunement of Planet Earth, and ensure that the highest possible timeline of our global destiny prevails over the ignorance of selfish tendencies currently gripping the planet.

A species-wide shift happens because the collective field is being fed and informed by the cresting wave of those souls at the bow of our evolutionary ship — souls such as you who are questing for the timeless truth! As we know, the immense tidal pull of the fear paradigm still rampant in humanity's collective psyche does not make surfing towards this new frontier an effortless ride. It demands an active command of our Higher Self, with a "motion of devotion" every moment to steer clear of the denser whirlpools of energies and thoughts and instead sail masterfully by using our spiritual compass. However, when we are truly in our Light, we drop the notion that we need to change anything and that there is even an "I" who is doing things, anyway. A singular focus on Truth and Self-Realization naturally unites all of our "personal" actions of dedication to the Light, with the greater upliftment of all beings. In a sense, you can't help but be part of the change if you are God-centered. It's the nature of the web!

(Amoraea is a visionary, wisdom teacher, soul awareness facilitator, and spiritual guide and is also the artist for the cover art of the *2012: Create Your Own Shift* book. Please visit his website www.Divine-Blueprint.com for a grand tour of all his gifts to humanity.)

Shifting the Power

by Drunvalo Melchizedek

Life is amazing! Every 13,000 years on Earth, a sacred and secret event takes place that changes everything — an event that changes the very course of history. And at this moment, this rare event is occurring right now, but only a few people know about it. And most of those who do know have kept it quiet and hidden until now.

What I am speaking about is the Earth's Kundalini. Connected to the center of the Earth is an energy that appears and behaves much like a snake as it moves, similar to the way Kundalini energy moves in the human body.

It is this energy that gives rise to the spiritual seekers everywhere on Earth — not only in the ashrams, kandas, and monasteries of the world, but also even in ordinary life and ordinary people who, in their own way, are seeking God. The Earth's Kundalini is the secret energy that is connected to the hearts of all of mankind.

The Earth's Kundalini is always attached to a single location on the surface of the Earth and stays there for a period of about 13,000 years. But then it moves to a new location for the next 13,000 years, based upon cycles of time, or what we call the Precession of the Equinoxes. And when it moves, our idea of what "spiritual" means changes. It transforms according to the new energies of the future cycle, leading us into a higher spiritual path.

The bigger picture is this: The Kundalini has two poles, and one is in the exact center of the Earth. The other is located on the surface somewhere and anywhere in the world. It is the consciousness of the Earth herself that decides where it is to be.

And there is a pulse of exactly 12,920 years when the polarity of the Earth's Kundalini changes to the opposite pole, and it simultaneously changes location on the surface of the Earth. This new location not only rapidly wakes up the people living near this sacred point on the Earth, but also it sends a frequency into the electromagnetic grids surrounding the Earth. This, in turn, affects those consciousness grids in ways that are determined by the Earth's DNA. We grow according to a set plan and design.

To the few that know of this event and what is occurring all around us, a wisdom is transferred and a peaceful state of being becomes their inheritance, for they know the awesome truth. In the midst of chaos, war, starvation, plagues, environmental crisis, and moral breakdown that we are all experiencing here on Earth today at the end of this cycle, they understand the transition and know no fear. This fearless state is the secret key to the transformation that, for millions of years, has always followed this secret cosmic event.

... On one level, this means that spiritually the female will now have her turn to lead mankind (womankind) into the New Light. And eventually, this female spiritual light will permeate the entire range of human experience from female leaders in business and religion to female heads of state. By 2012–2013 this female spiritual light will become so strong as to be obvious to all who live on this dear planet, and it will continue to grow for thousands of years.

... People from different cultures and countries are all cooperating together "as though" they were coordinated by a higher power simply for the good of human life. And without this spiritual assistance, I believe humanity would be unable to evolve to the next level of consciousness, crucial to our very survival.

For me, the call to this way of life was so strong that I felt like I had no choice. It simply began to happen all around me as I followed my inner guidance.

But I am not the only one. There are tens of thousands of people — mostly indigenous people — who have been led by a deep inner guidance, from 1949 to the present, to help to bring this unyielding White Snake to its new location high up in the Andes Mountains in Chile, where it now finally resides. Not only is this a shift of spiritual power from the male to the female, but it is also a spiritual power shift from Tibet and India to Chile and Peru. The light of the world that has been nurtured and expanded with the Tibetan and Indian cultures is now completed. Its new reign has just begun in Chile and Peru, and soon it will affect the hearts of all mankind.

... Like I said, Life is amazing!

(Reprinted with permission from the Introduction to Drunvalo's book, *Serpent of Light Beyond 2012: The Movement of the Earth's Kundalini and the Rise of the Female Light, 1949–2013.*)

The Rays in Relation to the Earth Changes

by The Elders (ancient celestial beings and High Council members of the Order of Melchizedek), through Anrita Melchizedek

Sweet Beings, it gives us great pleasure to be with you in this moment and to see the acceleration of the changes occurring, individually and collectively. Of course, Mother Earth is this mirror, in not only the clearings that she is going through (primarily working with the emotional body), but this reflection is creating many of the ascension symptoms that you are experiencing, individually and collectively. Further to this, not only is Mother Earth clearing — in a controlled manner — places within her energy field within which darker energies may exist, but the energy of the rays is assisting in creating change on this Earth plane.

The rays themselves can be described as Divine unfoldings of Light coming from the Cosmic Heart of Mother/Father God, each bringing the essence of the God Light, also known as Ein Soph. These rays — twelve great rays — spiral forth from the Cosmic Heart of Mother/Father God dimensionally through the stars and planets, until they enter this solar system, and from here — on planet Earth in particular — these rays are activated through Shamballa and the second Ray of Love-Wisdom before spiraling out onto this Earth plane, and the higher aspects to the rays amplifying the vortices and sacred sites on this Earth plane.

Now, you as a Soul, travel through the energy of the rays onto this Earth plane, often finding where you choose to be born, related to the energy of one of the rays that you are integrating in that lifetime. For each country falls under the influence of particular rays, with a predominant ray influence on that country. As the Earth herself is shifting in her magnitude, so the vibrations of the rays are changing from country to country, for the collective consciousness of each country holds the energy vibration that is imbued with both the higher and lower aspects of the related ray. What is happening with the energy of the rays in relation to the Earth, sweet ones, is that the higher aspects to the vibrational qualities of these rays (and in particular the vibrations of the eighth to the twelfth rays) are being activated and actualized on this Earth plane at this moment in time, leading up to 2012. The ashrams for these higher rays were built in 1994, and since this time these higher rays — rays eight to twelve — have been available for all

23

of humanity. They carry a higher quotient of Source Light and do not have the dualities inherent in the first seven rays. Many of the star children have come through, through the energy of these higher rays, and thus do not experience the level of duality that many of the older Light Workers have experienced in this lifetime.

Until the year 2012, you are going to experience the energy of each of these first twelve rays, and from this time, the Cosmic rays will hold more of a focus for Lightworkers in particular. (In 2010, the energy of the tenth ray of Divinity was experienced through the energy of Mother Earth. [This ray, overlighted by the energy of the Mahatma, the Cosmic Avatar of Synthesis, and one of the twelve Directors of these Cosmic Rays, brought through the perfect balance of the first ray of Will and Power, the second Ray of Love-Wisdom, and the third ray of Divine Intelligence, respectively. In fact all rays are created with the essence of these first three rays, also known as the three-fold flame of Power, Love, and Wisdom.]

The Earth itself falls under the energy of the third ray of Divine Intelligence. The lower aspect to the energy of this ray is about clearing and transmuting "the lesser-than and better-than consciousness." And to a lesser degree, the influence of the first ray of Will and Power, which carries with it in its lower aspects many of the power and control issues and victim/persecutor consciousness that are being perpetuated on this Earth plane. Through being able to lift yourself into the higher qualities of the third ray and the first ray respectively, taking yourself into the mind of God, and coming into empowerment as well as trusting and surrendering to the Divine, you lift yourself into the energy of the second ray of Love-Wisdom. And the balance of these three rays is to be found within the tenth ray of Divinity. This pearlescent flame is connected to the throat chakra, allowing you the utterance of your spiritual reality. As Mother Earth is experiencing her spiritual reality and lifting herself into the glorious state of ascension, so this is occurring for all life too, and in this balance you find for yourself between these first three rays is to be experienced in the utterance of your truth in expressing your true nature as a Spiritual Being of Light.

In 2011, the focus is on the eleventh ray of Illumined Truth, the most beautiful pearlescent flame of Divinity. That ray activates the Divine Feminine aspects of unconditional Love, compassion, insight and understanding, through the heart and third eye in particular. And in 2012, sweet ones, the focus will be on the twelfth ray of Divinity, this beautiful golden ray of Unity Consciousness.

Now proceeding further to the twelve earthly rays, there is a focus on the building of the ashrams for what we call the six Cosmic Rays, through these twelve rays that spiral forth from the Cosmic Heart of Mother/Father God, bringing through particular sonic vibrations, colors, qualities and geometries of light that are creating change, individually and collectively. As these rays travel from dimension to dimension, and within the system of energy that we work with from the ninth dimension to the third dimension, these rays are amplified with a focus of all twelve rays, and one or more of these rays, too. What this creates is a system of six Cosmic rays. We have been experiencing the energy of these six Cosmic rays as we shift into the deeper level of Christ Consciousness and for you, sweet beings, the understanding of these levels of Christ Consciousness takes you into what we call at this moment "Solar Christ Consciousness."

Solar Christ Consciousness takes you into the energy of the solar system, past the ring-pass-not that exists around the Earth plane into a higher vibration of Light, which will be experienced permanently from the year 2012–2013. This Solar Christ Consciousness vibration creates a thirteenth ray, or the first Cosmic ray, which is an amplification of all twelve rays and a higher light focus on the second ray of Love-Wisdom. In other words, all life is going to experience the energy of Love-Wisdom as you shift into a higher level of Light. Those souls that choose not to experience this vibrational energy of Love-Wisdom, or the thirteenth ray of Solar Service, will find themselves on a parallel Earth plane when they pass over, but this Earth and all life on her that chooses to ascend will experience this beautiful copper-gold flame of Solar Christ Consciousness. The energy of this ray is one of manifestation and it is being imbued in all life on this Earth plane with impulses of Light through the ashrams that are being built within Shamballa housing these qualities. These ashrams housing the six Cosmic rays will be complete by the years 2012-2013 and this will allow you to experience a cosmic map into the Cosmic Heart of Mother/Father God.

The energy of the rays not only brings through these qualities, colors, and sonic vibrations of Light, overlighted by particular Masters of the Light, but the energy of the rays is assisting you in stepping into self-mastery, and into becoming these Ascended Masters of Light. In stepping into the I Am Avatar Blueprints as these first wave Souls in human embodiment holding these encodings of Light, we honor and welcome you as these Master Beings of Love and Light, as these Keepers of Light to Mother Earth.

With this, we bid you a most magical day.

(For more information on Anrita Melchizedek, and The Melchizedek and Pleiadian Light Network, please view our website at www.pleiadianlight.net and You Tube channel at http://www.youtube.com/user/AnritaMelchizedek)

An Introduction to Change

by Justin Wilknson

Down through the ages, man has been asking the fundamental questions of his being: "Who am I?" and "Where did I come from?" These questions stem from inner, deep-seated roots that have poised us to strive forward, for a further comprehension of knowledge and wisdom.

In past millennia, the Greeks seemed to bring the light into the world with alchemy, poetry and democracy, furthering man's ability to freely express himself. Later, during the European Renaissance, the human consciousness experienced a great change in social expression. People suddenly had an immense urge to express themselves through creative music, art and theater. The whole world had never seen such creativity on a mass scale before that.

At the same time, the older political and religious laws of the Dark Ages seemed to no longer satisfy the more analytical and scientific minds. The outer objective changes that we can observe in those times were only reflections of that which was esoteric or inward. In other words, the changes we see are only symptoms.

The source responsible for these changes is important to discuss and embrace here, because it corresponds to the movement of our solar system through the constellations of the Zodiac, which is roughly a 26,000-year cycle. In approximately 1675, the energies of Pisces began to slowly withdraw from the world, and a new force began to enter. The energy of Aquarius is a very different energy because it is an expression of group consciousness, and is demonstrated through synthesis and cooperation.

Each constellation emits a certain frequency of energy — a certain quality of its particular characteristic. Each constellation can be seen as a Great Personality within a greater body, each with its own unique character. Our solar system is conditioned by these energies as it passes through them. During the Age of Pisces (which is now ending), the primary stream of influence on humanity was that of individuality and devotion to an ideal. This is what brought humanity out of the herd-like consciousness that had existed before. This stronger sense of individuality led people to question the authority of their kings and priests as being superior. This sense of "self" sparked an inner awareness in many, which the religious doctrines could not explain or reproduce. They had made God something separate from Man, as if it were some elusive, unreachable and unknowable entity that could only be reached through the Church.

As a new science began to develop, the world became polarized between conflicting ideologies. This struggle still persists today, yet in a more subtle form. However, with the advent of modern psychology, man has lifted yet another veil and is beginning to see his source. As the duality between religion and science is slowly being reconciled, more and more people are turning to metaphysics and newer ways of looking at the world. Man is beginning to access his higher mind as he progresses further down the path of evolution.

The new Age of Aquarius stands open before mankind. The Aquarian energies are permeating the world with greater potency now, and those energies support a new and different approach forward. The older Piscean energies of individual achievement are giving way to the Aquarian, unity consciousness. The world has shrunk in a technological and communications sense. Little happens that isn't known elsewhere or doesn't have an influence on the greater group of humanity.

The old institutions are crumbling to make way for new structures, which will inherently be better equipped to address the challenges that face mankind. These institutions will be much more sensitive to group cooperation among nations and cultures.

The playing field will be leveled, and no longer will the "haves" dictate the rules of the game to the "'have nots." There's no better example of this than the current global financial and economic crisis, as it demonstrates the unwinding of the old to prepare for the new. The unbridled greed and unregulated actions of the few have imploded upon themselves for the world to witness.

Circumstances and destiny have dictated a new start for a new age. The challenge will be to preserve those elements that have benefit to man, as opposed to scrapping everything simply for the sake of a different approach. This will take practical compromise and accommodation, as the world grapples with the new more humanitarian approaches. Mankind is ready. Our challenges and problems are never bigger than our ability to change, if we'll just align ourselves with Divine Will.

A point of crisis — a tipping point — has been reached, with the waters of the Age of Aquarius poised to flow freely. The water carrier awaits our beck and call. Prophecies have foretold these times. Whether Mayan,

Vedic, Christian, Hopi or many others, they have pointed to the end of this Age as a time that will usher in a new order.

The time line for the evolution of our consciousness is speeding up, being compressed into a tight timeframe to prepare us to embrace the changes we face. Mayan lore predicts that human consciousness will expand as much in the year 2012 as it has in the entire history of mankind. The outer world will reflect this explosion of consciousness in every possible way.

As man's inner awareness expands, outer circumstances will better reflect this new appreciation of the fundamental truth that we are "one." As individual expressions of the one great human Over-Soul, we are resonating with a collective realization that all is connected. The individual atoms, cells, and molecules of our dense physical bodies and of our more subtle etheric nature are all vibrating at a higher rate!

This date of 2012 is only the beginning of laying down the stepping stones into a new age. Many have come to prepare the way: Rama, Krishna, Mithra, Buddha, The Christ and Mohammed. All divine teachers have had a message and plan for their time and place. Today, the major religions expect a world teacher, whether it be the reappearance of The Christ, Krishna, Maitreya, Buddha, the Imam Mahdi, or the Messiah. At a time least expected, he will appear, but probably not the way we expect. Master DK (Dwhal Khul) says that the World Teacher (The Christ) may come in physical form, but that as a precondition, the hearts and minds of men must be expressing his love and wisdom. Mankind must be taking the right steps, moving in the right direction, with a measure of peace prevailing.

Mankind can go kicking, screaming and suffering into the Golden Age, or we can make the individual choices and take the collective actions that will smooth our transition into our awaiting destiny. The time is short and the stakes are high. As the *Mayan Cosmogenesis* describes, the earth will be in direct alignment with the center of our galaxy by the year 2012, an event that hasn't happened in about 26,000 years. The Light of God will be more intense than at any time in the history of man. What we do with that Light remains to be seen.

(Justin Wilkinson has produced many videos and maintains these recommended sites:

http://www.ponderonthis.net and http://www.theaglesswisdom.net)

"We are literally transforming our bodies from one form into another as our planet undergoes her own transformational process at the same time." — *Dawn Newton*

The 2012 Phenomena: The Transformation of Humanity and their Planet

by Dawn Newton —Transformer/Contactee

We are literally transforming our bodies from one form into another as our planet undergoes her own transformational process at the same time. Each is connected to the other, as we are not separate from one another as individuals, nor are we separate from our planet. She is as much a part of our body as we are a part of hers.

What the ancient healing modality of acupuncture identifies as energetic meridians within the human body, Mother Earth's meridians are identified as the magnetic grid. According to the ancient teachings of the Hindu, our bodies collect energetic/magnetic information (quantum physics) via miniature transformer/transmitters within the body, called chakras. For eons of time, these chakras kept us in alignment and attuned with our planet's magnetic grid via a Chakra System, in which there were a total of 12 chakras. These mini-computers would then disseminate this information throughout the body via 12 strands of DNA, in order for us to "Know Thy Self."

Humanity's Original Image

Eons ago, when we first arrived on this planet, we came in the original I Am image of Source Energy. We came in highly sensitive bodies, with 12 strands of DNA and 12 chakras, which aligned with our planet Earth's energetics. We were connected to her as one entity: as above so below. Our energetics were in synch for eons of time, and we lived for hundreds of years at one time, acquiring vast amounts of experiential gnosis and wisdom. Human Beings were not the only Beings who walked upon the planet, however; our Star families also walked amongst us.

Deconstructing the Original I Am Image

As time moved onwards, the Human Beings and Star Beings began to war for power over one another, and soon we were battling not only here on Earth but throughout our universe. What eventually took place was the dismantling of our communication systems — within our own body, with one another, and with our planet — and we fell into the 3D plane of existence, searching for the meaning to life with very few circuits of our energy cords operating. We were disconnected from 10 strands of our DNA, which closed down several chakras on our body. Our planet suffered from this disconnect, as well , as one energy fed upon the other because we kept each other centered and balanced. Subsequently, she too, began to weaken — so much so she began to tilt on her axis, indicating she was a cancerous "cell," if you will, in the body of Goddess God, of which it is that we are representative of here in this universe.

Rebuilding The I Am Presence/Image: Dawning of the Age of Aquarius

Currently, Human Beings have been undergoing a profound recon-struction period from 1999 thru 2012. Humanity and our planet have not only survived, but are once again coming into alignment with our original I Am image, after our planet had journeyed over 26,000 years through her galactic cycle. This journey has brought her and her inhabitants to the end of an era of disconnect, where collectively each were "stuck on stupid." This phase of our existence — the Piscean Age — has come to an end. Our collective movement throughout our galaxy has once again brought us into alignment with a time-space-continuum portal, known as the Aquarian Age! The only way for us to make it through this Doorway/Portal is via our frequency — our original I Am Frequency, which is not a 3D vibration. Thus, humanity is upgrading — reconnecting to our other 10 strands of DNA, as well as reopening the 5 closed chakras, in order to become a higher frequency or resonance. This transformation is causing humanity to suffer through some pretty intense body changes, known as ascension symptoms.

Ascension Symptoms: Human and Earth

As humanity begins to transform, the body itself is sloughing off, cleansing, and purging all matter of maladies — illnesses of every stripe, that have no specific diagnosis that can be attached to them: headache, earache, sinus attack, cold sore, diarrhea, boils, sties, digestive problems, lack of appetite, can't sleep, can't stay awake, and electrical types of sensations throughout the body — as these new circuits are reconnected once again. These are just the physical upgrades. We are also undergoing emotional, mental and spiritual upgrades, causing us to awaken on a level akin to a new Golden Age of Awareness. Our planet is also sloughing off, cleansing, and purging herself, as she begins to realign with her original I Am image through her magnetic grid. Thus, since 1999, Planet Earth's changes (ascension symptoms) have increased, causing tsunamis, hurricanes, tornados, floods, and volcanic activity. These have been felt around the globe with the least amount of death ever thought possible from the magnitude of such dramatic Earth rumblings.

Why We Are Here During This Transformation

The only reason we are here right now is to help one another to ascend through this time-space-continuum portal. We are Transformers; we have come to transform ourselves from 3D entities into our Original Image, so that we can return to Source Energy (if we so choose) once we ascend from the 3D plane of "stuck on stupid." We each had a plan before arriving here; as did Jesus. His was a human life example, a template we all are meant to replicate. Thus, we come with a set plan at the ready to help humanity ascend into higher states of awareness. In that state of higher awareness, the body arises into another plane of existence, beyond the 3D plane, just as Jesus said we could also do: "Even these things and greater shall ye do." What is your Divine Purpose? What did you come to share in order to move humanity and this planet through that portal?

(Dawn Newton is the author of *I Saw A Mountain Move Today: Ascending from Victim to Divine Purpose*, to be released in 2011. You can find her on Facebook.)

"Are we in the eleventh hour of this 3D game? The frequency of seeing those little 11:11 wakeup calls sure seems to hint that we are. Actually, I'd guess that we're more like in the last 11 seconds of the 11th hour. However, what's coming isn't ever nearly as important as what is right now." — Hunt Henion

11:11, 12.21.12 & 13:13

By Hunt Henion

Clocks I see lately always seem to have triple digits on them, and I'm seeing these triple digits (4:44, 5:55, etc.), as well as 11:11, everywhere and all the time these days. How is that possible?

There are clues to the nature of things to be found in mythology. The ancient Egyptian version of the Alpha and Omega (beginning and ending), is one being they called Atum (Ra). According to the old teachings, our goal is to become more god-like, and Atum began the becoming. His name literally means "all" and "nothing," "beginning and ending."

In these ancient teachings, the philosophy of the oneness of all things (and nothing), combined with a profound, simultaneous beginning and ending, is actually pretty inescapable.

Today, we also have computers as a reminder of this oneness. One is, of course, "the beginning," but in computer talk of zeros and ones, one means "the end." 11 therefore, might mean both, the beginning and ending. 11:11 seems to reinforce that by representing the two meanings with two 11s. Also, no matter how you look at it, forward or backward, we have a simultaneous "beginning and ending." Two elevens also seem to hint at a reference to our dualistic world. If we were little bits of information or code in the program of life, 11:11 might be thought of as the glitch that gives us a peek at the rest of the program.

This is all guesswork, but 11:11 does seem to jump right out at you. Just like when someone calls your name, it wakes you up. And once we begin to be conscious of it, it fills us with wonder.

Are we in the eleventh hour of this 3D game? The frequency of seeing those little 11:11 wakeup calls sure seems to hint that we are.

Actually, I'd guess that we're more like in the last 11 seconds of the 11th hour. However, what's coming isn't ever nearly as important as what is right now. For many, the future — like all unknowns — throws them into the trap of fear. Sometimes it's better not to prophesy, but just look at the wondrous changes in the works — in the world, and in ourselves.

Generally, people are getting more communicative and sensitive in exactly the way many believe the ancient Mayans predicted. The presence of 11:11 in our consciousness seems like an element, or a least a symbol, of this new communication.

The Long Count of the Mayan Calendar ends on December 21, 2012 (12.21.12). According to the Navy's Astronomical Applications Department, the winter solstice on 12.21.2012 will begin at exactly at 11:11 A.M.! I suppose it could be coincidence, but it sure feels like another of those increasingly frequent hints or reminders that we're all part of something much bigger than anything we know, so perhaps we fit into cycles we're just beginning to understand.

On December 21, 2012, the north pole of the rotational axis of the Earth will begin to point to the edge of the section of space that we've come to call Aquarius. This will be the actual beginning of The Age of Aquarius, a time of peace and enlightenment that will last for 2,160 years. Then, there are five more astrological houses that also promise peace and prosperity.

It seems that as long as the Earth's axis points *toward* the center of the galaxy, which it does for half the trip around the Precession of the Equinoxes (or about 13,000 years), it's like standing in the sunlight, as enlightenment fills our consciousness.

Then, as the Earth's axis begins to point away from the center of the galaxy, mankind seems to fall asleep spiritually, and things become more negative. At the 26,000-year mark (after one complete trip around the Precession of the Equinoxes), serious disruption almost always occurs. Still, that disruptive impact is just a speed bump compared to what happens at the end of a cycle that's 1000 times larger.

Two paleontologists, David Raup and John Sepkoski, wrote an abstract published in 1984 by the National Academy of Sciences called, "Periodicity of Extinctions in the Geologic Past." They studied 12 extinction events. "The 12 events show a statistically significant periodicity ($P < 0.01$) with a mean interval between events of 26 million years." In other words, science is aware of 12 extinction events in our past that occur about every 26 million years. They go on to say that meteorites only caused two of them, but they suspect that there are some more basic cyclical causes, "related to extraterrestrial forces (solar, or galactic)."

Stepping down this 26-million-year cycle a bit, we find that the Earth's Precession of the Equinoxes, which is the time it takes the Earth to make a complete circle in the sky (as traced by the north pole of its axis of rotation), is about 26,000 years.

If we look back 26,000 years ago to when the Earth was pointed in the exact same direction as it is now, we see that Cro-Magnon man roamed the Earth. Stepping this cycle down further, it's interesting to consider that perhaps the 260-day gestation period for a human in the womb correlates to a 26,000 year gestation period of a human species.

It's also interesting that so many believe that a new sort of human is developing right now. Many have been talking for years about the special abilities of what they call the Indigo or Crystal children. The Incan elders have also recently announced the emergence of what they call "Homo luminous." Some people are quick to point out the differences in the extraordinary abilities of the children they observe. However, the point here is that people are suddenly, and for the most part unexplainably, changing.

Paul Dong and Thomas E. Raffill wrote a book in 1997 entitled *China's Super Psychics*. It documents studies of children who demonstrated an ability to see flawlessly with their ears, nose, mouth, hands or feet. *Omni* magazine did its own follow-up on this. They went over there, took a page out of a book at random, crumpled it up, and put it in the armpit of one of the psychic kids, who then read every word on that page. Their report on their study was released in their January 1985 issue.

My favorite story in the *China's Super Psychics* book is the account of an audience of several thousand who were all given a rosebud before taking their seat. A little six-year-old girl walks out on stage, waves her hand and all the rosebuds open up simultaneously.

A March 7, 2006 *New York Times* article, "Still Evolving, Human Genes Tell New Story," written by Nicholas Wade, begins: "Providing the strongest evidence yet that humans are still evolving, researchers have detected some 700 regions of the human genome where genes appear to have been reshaped …"

Western researchers have generally only been interested in the 10% of our DNA that regulates biological and emotional traits. They call the other 90% — which includes those parts that have been identified as having been "reshaped" — "junk DNA." Yet, this "junk" has been recently shown to respond to thought, intent and sound, all of which brings us back to the "intelligent design" theory that was thrown out shortly after Darwin made his debut.

In *The Science of Peace*, Dr. Glen Rein demonstrates how negative emotion causes DNA to contract, while positive emotion causes it to expand, which enhances healing.

Examples of how DNA responds to thought and words are as endless as the examples of how humans are very quickly evolving in ways that take our experience of the world to a whole new level.

Dr. Rein's research into how emotional states affect our very DNA makes me wonder about the implications of some classic psychological advice (loosely translated): "The most important things to have are faith, hope and love; and the greatest of these is love."

I don't think I've ever heard better guidance on how to prepare for the new, evolved world than that! It comes from I Corinthians 13:13. Hmmmm… Do you suppose that chapter and verse could be a clue to anything — an intelligent presence, a cycle, a powerful unseen causality of some sort?

11:11 stimulates our imagination and hope, just as these times test what we really choose to see and believe. 11:11, 13:13, and 12.21.12 may mean nothing to some people. To others, they may be symbols of the doorway to a greater reality. To a few of those, the faith, hope and love that those symbols inspire will be found to be reliable keys to that doorway to the infinite.

I've heard kids say, "It's "time to make a wish," when they see 11:11 or repetitive numbers on a clock. "Out of the mouths of babes …"

I don't know exactly what's going to happen at the end of the Mayan Calendar any more than I know what's going to happen at 11:11 today. However, my wishes are ready!

(Excerpted from the award-winning book, *The Big Fake-out: The Illusion of Limits*, by Hunt Henion www.shiftawareness.com)

The Journey Back to Self: THE RETURN

by the Arcturians, channeled by Suzanne Lie, Ph.D.

We, the Arcturians, wish to inform you that 2012 is the end of the beginning and the beginning of an end. It is the end of the beginning of the Aquarian Age and the beginning of the fulfillment of the 2012 prophecies. It is also the beginning of the end of living in a polarized reality.

2012 is not just a date. It is a process of completing a cycle. You started this cycle about 26,000 years ago, when your current Precession of the Equinoxes began. At that "time," you were starting the process of separating from your reality of living in Unity with the ONE. Therefore, you had no way of knowing how very lost your Soul could become after myriad incarnations in a progressively dualistic world.

The long journey from your Home in the womb of the ONE, which you were just leaving, to the Galactic Womb, to which you are returning, was to be more sorrowful and lonely than you could have ever imagined. Furthermore, you had no way of knowing that you would forget your Home in the ONE, and since you forgot it, you had no way of returning.

Interestingly enough, the very "time" that you did not know existed, prior to your journey into an increasingly dualistic reality, became the key to your return Home to the Fifth Dimension and beyond. You discovered that once you could release your third-dimensional concept of time, you could begin to embrace the NOW of the ONE.

Within the NOW, the ONE began to speak to you as the still, small voice within. At first, you could not imagine that the voice was you, for how could YOU have such a wise, loving voice? Often this inner guidance differed from that which you heard in your outer world, but you felt the unconditional love that carried the message into your consciousness. It was this unconditional love that allowed you to listen to this voice over the many internal and external voices of fear and judgment.

This love without conditions gave you the courage to look deeper inside for that which you could not find in your daily life. Your inner messages often came in flashes of enlightenment that took years or decades to understand, but the resonance of unconditional love allowed you to accept these messages even though you often could not understand or utilize them.

As your inner voice settled deeper into your consciousness, you learned that in order to understand it, you needed to surrender into its Knowing. This Knowing taught you that this voice was actually a higher frequency of your own Multidimensional SELF. Your SELF told you that in order to complete your cycle and return to the ONE, you had to expand your consciousness to BE your true SELF in your daily life.

As your consciousness continued to expand, your belief that you were a great, Multidimensional Being allowed you to expect to perceive a higher resonance of life. Because your belief directs your expectations and your expectations direct your perceptions, you began to perceive a higher resonance of reality. Since the reality you perceive is the reality you live, your conscious journeys into the higher dimensions began.

With each journey, you began to download more and more of your Multidimensional SELF into your consciousness and your physical body. These downloads expanded your Personal Consciousness to embrace the Collective Consciousness, and eventually, the Planetary Consciousness. In this manner, your awakening to "being your SELF" in daily life progressed.

At first, just a few of you awakened. Then, more and more awakened every day. Those of you who were awakened to your true, multidimensional nature began to share your story to assist others to awaken, as well. That which had so terrified you in the darkness of your long night of forgetfulness was revealed by the increasing dawn to be only an illusion. One by one, your illusions of separation were released, which expanded your consciousness even further into Galactic Consciousness. Because you remembered that YOU were the planet, then the galaxy became your family.

No longer could you harm another, as you saw every person as ONE with your SELF. No longer could you harm your planet or any of her inhabitants, for you saw them as ONE with your SELF. No longer could you fear extraterrestrials, for you remembered that they were members of your Galactic Family.

Your concept of SELF expanded beyond being "just a person," for you were ONE with ALL life. It was then that your most difficult challenge began. Your ever-expanding consciousness reminded you that you were not just ONE with that which you loved and respected, for if you were ONE with all life, then you were also ONE with that which you feared and judged. In 2012, you must ALL remember that unconditional love is UNCONDITIONAL!

As 2012 approaches, person and planet are returning to the Galactic Center to complete their joint process of ascension. The torsion waves emanating from the Galactic Center resonate to Multidimensional Light, Unconditional Love and Divine Creativity. These waves are expanding your perception of your Multidimensional SELF more and more each day. Meanwhile, your inner voice is constantly reminding you to BE your SELF in your daily life.

Every day you, people and planet, are absorbing more of these torsion waves, which are activating new codes in your personal and planetary DNA. Because of this, your personal and planetary bodies are changing, and your consciousness is expanding into Cosmic Consciousness. You are remembering that YOU are ONE with the planet, the solar system, the galaxy and the universe. No longer can you diminish yourself or do what you dislike. No longer can you allow another to command your life. No longer can you believe that you are separate from the planet, the galaxy or the cosmos through which you travel.

We, the Arcturians, wish you to Know that YOU, person and planet, are returning Home to your fifth-dimensional expression of SELF. It is this Knowing that allows you to believe that your Light resonates far beyond the fear that once imprisoned you. In the Fifth Dimension and beyond, unconditional love is the constant light message that forever caresses your great Being. 2012 is the process of healing ALL fear with the very unconditional love that first aroused you from your slumber. It is this unconditional love that will guide you HOME.

2012 is not a "time." It is a "process of returning HOME."

That process is occurring NOW!

(The Arcturians, through Suzanne Lie, Ph.D.
www.multidimensions.com and www.suzanliephd.com)

"You cannot change your frequency or vibration immediately; it would be too strong and would destroy your body. It has to be done in stages. Many of us can sense on another level of our being that something is happening. With the changes subtly going on around us, our physical bodies must also change in order to adjust."
— *Dolores Cannon*

Planetary Transformation: The Coming New Earth

by Dolores Cannon

And I saw a new heaven and a new earth, for the first heaven and the first earth were passed away ... — Revelation 21:1

My research in the field of hypnosis has taken me on unimaginable journeys through time and space to explore the history of the past and the possibilities of the future. When I first began my investigations through past life therapy, I thought I would only find people remembering lives on Earth, because naturally that was all we knew about.

My belief system has really been stretched and extended over the past 30 years. As my work progressed, I was given a great deal of information about the beginning of life on Earth. I was told that this is the time for this knowledge to come forth. We are moving into a new world, a new dimension, where this information will be appreciated and applied.

During my work, I have heard much about everything being composed of energy; the shape and form is only determined by the frequency and vibration. Energy never dies; it only changes. I have been told that the Earth is changing its vibration and frequency and preparing to rise into a new dimension. There are countless dimensions surrounding us all the time. We cannot see them because as the vibrations speed up, they are invisible to our eyes. It is important for us to know more about this shift to a new dimension because it is coming soon.

Earth is a school that we go to and learn lessons, but it is not the only school. You have lived on other planets and in other dimensions. You have done many, many things you cannot even imagine. Many of the people I have worked with in the last few years have regressed to lifetimes where they were light beings living in a state of bliss. They had no reason to come into the Earth's density and negativity. They volunteered to come to help mankind and the Earth at this time. I have encountered what I consider to be three waves of these new souls who are living on Earth. They have come at this time because most of those who have been here for lifetime after lifetime have become bogged down in karma and are not advancing. They have lost sight of the purpose for being here.

The first wave of these souls, now in their late 40s to early 60s, had the most difficult time adjusting. They didn't like the violence and ugliness they found in this world and wanted to return "home" — even though they had no conscious idea where that might be. The second wave is now in their late 20s and early 30s. They are moving through life much too easily. They are generally focused on helping others, creating no karma, and normally going unnoticed. The third wave is the new children, many of whom are now in their teens. They have come in with all the knowledge needed, on an unconscious level. Their DNA has already been altered and they are prepared to proceed with little or no problems.

THE SIGNIFICANCE OF 2012

The question has been asked whether there will be a fourth wave. It will not be necessary, because something else is going to happen: we are moving into a New Earth — the first time it has ever happened in the history of the universe. Many civilizations have perished down through history because of man. Atlantis was one example, but there were many others. Each of these civilizations had tremendous advances. They had psychic abilities; they could do anything with their minds. The men of those times wanted more — power and greed — so eventually they violated the laws of the universe and they had to be brought down. Each time this happened, some humans were left to start civilization over again. This has happened time after time after time.

… Many civilizations have disappeared from the Earth without a trace. Among these are the Mayans, the Anasazi, and many others. During regressions, I have had people go back to those times. Each of these ancient cultures evolved spiritually to a point that their entire civilization moved into a higher dimension. The Mayans saw that the next great advancement was going to be when the entire world would shift into a higher dimension. This is what they saw happening in 2012. It is not the end of the world; it is when the entire world moves into a new dimension.

The transition began around 2003. The culmination is going to be in 2012. Time is speeding up. Earth's frequencies and vibrations are changing. But not everyone is going to go, just as it says in the Bible: "Then two shall be in the field; the one will be taken, the other left." It is very real. When the transformation reaches its peak in 2012, the energy becomes so strong that it will push the Earth into the new dimension. There will not be anything dramatic; it will be very subtle, very slow, and only those who are really aware will know anything is happening. Things will look different and feel different. The old Earth is where we are going to have all the catastrophes, and these are going to increase because the Earth is lifting itself as it shifts.

You cannot change your frequency or vibration immediately; it would be too strong and would destroy your body. It has to be done in stages. Many of us can sense on another level of our being that something is happening. With the changes subtly going on around us, our physical bodies must also change in order to adjust. Some of these physical symptoms are unpleasant and cause concern. Just be aware of what is happening: the body is adjusting and adapting to different energy levels so it can move on.

(The above was taken from the *Light Of Consciousness* magazine, Vol. 22, No. 2, Summer 2010. Dolores Cannon is a hypnotherapist who specializes in past life regressions. For the past 30 years, through her clients, she has been receiving messages from extraterrestrial entities about what we can expect as we near 2012.)

" ... as microcosms of Earth, you naturally are affected by the magnitude of changes the Earth is undergoing. Everything in your world is in acceleration mode, and there are frequent increases in the vibratory level along Earth's pathway; you still may be adjusting to the most recent level while she is moving into the next." — Matthew, channeled by Suzanne Ward

Matthew's Message

channeled by Suzanne Ward

Many Earth residents perceive your world as tumultuous as ever. Wars continue and so do poverty, corruption, oppression and other ills, so it is understandable that people who have long lived in such conditions often feel hopeless. You know that changes of unprecedented magnitude are afoot, yet you may be encountering unsettling feelings too, perhaps depression, discontentment, undue impatience, fatigue or physical discomfort. You may feel restless, "rudderless," floating without clear purpose or direction, or feel that nothing of significance is happening in your life or even anywhere on Earth.

It may be because world transformation is so far underway that many are having one or another of those sensations — as microcosms of Earth, you naturally are affected by the magnitude of changes the Earth is undergoing. Everything in your world is in acceleration mode, and there are frequent increases in the vibratory level along Earth's pathway; you still may be adjusting to the most recent level while she is moving into the next. Vibrations in the energy planes your planet has reached make maintaining balance in body, mind and spirit a greater effort than previously. When you are in a state of imbalance, your energy flow is jolted or blocked, causing your electromagnetic system to malfunction and produce a variety of unsettling physical, mental and emotional sensations.

Another effect of the higher vibrations is inner stirrings of dissatisfaction with personal situations. Individuals who are following intuitive feelings to change locations or work or relationships are faring better than those who are resisting soul-level guidance to get on track with karmic experiencing chosen to complete third density lifetimes.

The vibrations also are magnifying human characteristics and behaviors, making "good" better and "bad" worse. Generous persons share until the cupboard is bare, and those with warm hearts serve wherever help is needed. Greedy ones acquire more and more and give nothing, and heartless individuals cause problems for others. Played out on the world stage, light-filled people are thriving spiritually and activities of light nature are ever expanding in scope and positive results. People whose attributes and deeds are of darkness are regressing spiritually and their intentions and efforts are stumbling along into eventual futility. Interaction with individuals in the latter group can indeed be stressful because your light body's energy is resisting theirs.

A possible source of anomalous sensations and behaviors is Earth's ascension route, which puts her in new alignments with the other planets and Sol (our solar system's sun). Although the juxtaposition of solar bodies has always affected Earth's residents, the difference now is her rapid, steady course out of third density. Not only your feelings, but others' attitudes and reactions, which seem to be erratic, irresponsible or shocking may be due in part to unusual celestial influences.

The increase in geophysical activity is another potential source of stressful feelings because your bodies are affected by Earth's shockwaves. Another consideration here is that earthquakes, volcanic eruptions, violent storms and floods are relieving the negativity that caused the planet to spiral downward and, until about seventy or so years ago, had confined it for millennia to third density. The lessening of negativity also has an effect on bodies.

Let us digress a moment to answer a pertinent question: How much of the drastic weather and earthquakes and other "natural" disasters are man-made? It would not be much of an exaggeration to say "all." Just as in Nature, a technologically-created earthquake, for example, cannot have isolated effects — the energy release initiates activity in similarly vulnerable areas around the globe and those trigger still more upheavals. It is the same with clouds and winds. Mother Nature, however, knows when to take a time-out, so her lands and seas and skies can settle and she can regain balance, and she spares areas meant to be safe. The ones who are manipulating your weather and generating geophysical disasters don't care about healing respites for Earth or any exclusion from destruction, death toll and suffering.

Returning to possible causes for unpleasant symptoms that you may be experiencing, we offer practical suggestions to lessen their effects and duration. Fatigue never is your ally; get sufficient relaxation and sleep. Drinking a lot of pure water will help energy flow more smoothly throughout your body and let your electromagnetic system better perform. Physical and mental exercise, meditation, solitude, being in Nature, positive thinking, creative projects, melodious music — all are aids in balancing your energy.

Your bodies need light-filled foods for a strong immune system; eat more fresh fruits and vegetables and less meat and sugar. Illegal synthetic drugs, chemicals in prescription medications and alcohol not only are barriers to light absorption, they exacerbate the conditions you want to remedy and can create new types of dis-ease. Make every effort to avoid or defuse abrasive encounters — the energy those generate is a formidable deterrent to achieving balance and well-being. If, despite employing these suggestions and any other practices that usually have served you well, your symptoms become severe and persistent, please consult a trusted healthcare provider.

Now then, with the combination of that wide variety of energetic influences, the obvious turmoil in your world and unawareness of profound changes taking shape, it is little wonder that some believe the "end times" are coming and others interpret December 2012 (when the Mayan calendar ends) much the same way. Both perceptions are wrong, but indeed an end time is coming — along Earth's ascension pathway into the era of the Golden Age, all forms of darkness on the planet will end.

There are many questions and misconceptions about ascension, who will accompany Earth, what will become of the people who don't, and what to expect in the higher densities. First, ascension has nothing whatsoever to do with the "raptures" of any religion, so please do not try to fit that concept into the universal truth. Ascension is the process of Earth leaving third density and traveling through fourth on to fifth. Although this movement is into planes of successively lighter energy, not into progressively higher elevations such as climbing a stepladder or a mountain, souls' growth in conscious awareness and spiritual clarity can be thought of as upward, thus ascension is the most descriptive term for this advancement.

In the timeless continuum, the beginning and completion of Earth's ascension cannot be dated. You could say that both "times" have been known for untold ages. In linear time, the ascension process began in the last years of the 1930s, when atrocities long committed by humankind against each other reached unconscionable measure and nearly depleted Earth's light — that is, the life force of her planetary body and the bodies of all her residents.

Her cry for help went out into the universe and instantly God authorized myriads of spiritually advanced civilizations to respond by beaming their own vast light into Earth's body. The massive infusion of light from those distant sources stabilized Earth's orbit and enabled her to jar loose from negativity's stranglehold, start to ascend out of deep third density and continue toward her ultimate destination in fifth density. Her soul originated in that high plane and there it remained throughout the millennia during which her body spiraled ever downward as more and more human and animal blood was shed and the environment ravaged.

Ascension is possible for all who have absorbed the light, and the souls who accompany Earth will do so in their physical bodies. If bodies lack organs or limbs or have physical, emotional or mental disorders, farther along the ascension pathway there will be healing of all disease and replacement of missing parts until the bodies are perfected and mental and emotional health is sound. In fourth density, the bodies of aged persons will become youthful and live healthfully for much longer than your current life expectancy, and life spans in fifth density can be tenfold or more than yours are now.

There is no seat of judgment or arbitrary selection of which humans can ascend and which cannot; it is strictly a matter of science and souls' own choices. Light changes third-density's carbon-based cellular structure to the crystalline form that lets bodies survive in the higher frequencies, or vibrations, of fourth density and beyond. That is why persons who choose to live in the light can ascend with Earth and those who choose to cling to their dark ways cannot. After a time in spirit, souls in the latter group will incarnate in a world that corresponds to their Earth lifetime energy registration and have more opportunities to "see the light."

Not all light-filled people will go all the way to the Golden Age. It depends on the longevity clause in soul contracts. Prior to birth, many of today's populace chose to enter spirit life before Earth reaches that era, and among them are highly evolved souls whose light is as bright as the noonday sun. Those who came from higher civilizations to assist Earth in special ways during her ascension may quickly pass through Nirvana on their way to a higher-density spirit world, most likely the one serving their original homeland, or they may manifest new bodies and incarnate in another civilization for different kinds of growth-experiencing. Others will stay for a time in Nirvana, which will remain Earth's spirit world and ascend in tandem with the planet. Souls who have completed third-density karmic lessons may choose another Earth lifetime or join a civilization in a different fourth-density world.

A large number of people who have lived in godly ways will choose not to ascend with Earth after the truth about the origin of religions emerges: They were designed in darkness to deceive and control the people, to be the most divisive element of life on Earth, and to reap wealth for the heads of churches. Although everyone on Earth knows that truth at a soul level and it is a contract choice to consciously remember it, many of the devoutly religious will be unable or unwilling to accept that their deep-seated faith is founded on false teachings. By so doing, these individuals deny the light within truth, that they are god- and goddess-selves, eternally inseparable from God and all other souls in this universe. Their next pre-birth contract will again include the provision to become consciously aware of that truth during their next physical lifetime, which will be in a third-density world.

Regardless of the reason a soul leaves this lifetime, physical death will come from any of the many causes that exist now. There will be no mass departure of darkly inclined persons when Earth reaches some specific vibratory level, because the amount of light within bodies varies. And there is no way for you to distinguish between light-filled individuals who leave Earth in accordance with soul contracts, those who choose to leave rather than accept the truth about religions, and persons whose body's viability is snuffed out because they lack the light to survive in the vibratory level Earth entered.

In most cases there can be reunions of souls who live in physical or spirit worlds of differing densities. Those who have evolved into a higher density can astrally travel to a lower density that has sufficient light to assure the visitor's departure. Reunions are not possible with the souls that are consigned by their lifetime energy to first- or second-density worlds, where intelligence is almost nonexistent and no memories or feelings exist. That is not punishment; it offers those souls a new beginning free of the negativity they created that automatically led them to those lowest levels of existence.

The innocence of animals (who act from instinct, never from malice) automatically qualifies all except a few species to ascend with Earth. Along the way, those who now are wild will become tame, predators will become vegetarians, and all will live peaceably with each other and humankind. Already there is evidence of cross-species friendship, even mothers of one species nurturing infants of another, and instances of bonding between wild animals and humans.

Animal numbers will shrink in the next few years, as instinctively they will breed less often and produce fewer offspring. While most species will be able to adapt to environmental and climate changes as Earth is restored to her Eden self (when there were no temperature extremes and all lands were arable), species living in polar regions will not survive. Their souls will go to Nirvana and continue evolving, and in time they will incarnate in a world where conditions are suitable for their new bodies and life purposes.

Now then, despite the emphasis on the final day of year 2012, there is no absolutely fixed date for Earth to be within fourth density. There is a "celestial window" for smooth sailing, so to speak, but it offers a degree of flexibility in your calendar's time. And please remember that ascension is a process that has been ongoing for about seven decades, so do not expect a dramatic occurrence to herald the first day of the Golden Age. January 1, 2013 — often considered to be The Date — will be little different from the day preceding or following it. There is no validity to the notion that immediately prior to Earth's entry into fourth density, there will be three days of darkness or, as other reports have it, three days of burning sun.

It is not so that life after 2012 will be much the same throughout many centuries. Just as life on Earth has not been static, but has progressed through many phases of development, so too will life in the Golden Age. The difference is that everything will be taking place in the peace, harmony and boundless opportunities for learning and evolving in that glorious world! [The message dated December 31, 2007, "Essay on 2012" gives a comprehensive description of life in that era.]

The last phases of the transition from third density to fourth will present some challenges as the Illuminati keep trying to stir up trouble spots. Heeding your intuition will carry you through the bumpy episodes, which can't last much longer anyway because the dark ones cannot fight in the light, and the light is growing stronger by the day.

You don't consciously remember that you were eager to take on human form during this momentous time on Earth, and although many, many others also wanted to participate, they lacked the innate abilities, experience and courage that qualified you to be among the chosen. Few can be in prominent leadership roles, but all of you are leaders simply by being the shining god sparks you are! Do not for a moment doubt that you are powerful souls whose contributions to the light are helping assure its triumph over darkness. In the continuum, you already are victorious!

None of the dire situations that some analysts and some channeled messages purport to be likely, or even unavoidable, will come to pass. There will be no repeat of "9/11," no Third World War, no nuclear war in space, no worldwide riots because of food shortages, no inundation of coastlines until the seas reach the mountains, no pandemics or lack of drinking water that will imperil or eradicate billions of lives, no invasion by a dark civilization, no planetary destruction that will necessitate mass evacuations or underground living.

Hatonn asked us to give you his message: "My job as manager of communication between Earth and all other points in the universe is difficult enough. Please don't compound it by passing on false information or predictions that are pure hogwash. Thank you."

Some within the lightworker community are dismayed because the presence of other civilizations has not been officially acknowledged and no craft have landed. If we knew when the announcement will take place and when ships will land, we would happily tell you, but even our best sources for that information don't know. Your space family members living among you are eager to introduce themselves and the thousands in the spacecraft want to be on the ground helping you, but they must wait for the right time. The Illuminati's diversionary tactics have kept Earth's representatives preoccupied with major upheavals that have precluded final decisions about a televised announcement, and there can be no landings until your safety is fully assured. At this time, the Illuminati control weaponry poses a risk of danger to large numbers of people, and no chances will be taken with your lives.

Although there are optimistic indications of economic recovery, any improvements are purely by manipulation. The longstanding corruption in banking, investments and commerce cannot remain hidden much longer, nor can the usurious interest rates and unfair taxation continue; the Illuminati's worldwide economic network is crumbling irremediably. Your monetary system will return to precious metals as its basis, until such time that your heightened consciousness no longer requires the use of money in exchange for goods and services.

Concerns about current homelessness and unemployment are natural and so are ponderings about what will be the lot of homecoming troops if all military forces in the world are disbanded. Those concerns would vanish in the blink of an eye if you could see as we do the peace and joy, the harmony and cooperation, the abundance of life's necessities and enjoyments of Earth's Golden Age. Not only are lighted souls throughout the universe cheering you all along your pathway to that glorious world — we see you living there!

(The above was channeled on 8/12/10 by Suzanne Ward, author of the Matthew Books, www.matthewbooks.com.)

"Life seems to be a series of unconnected events, but in fact they are all connected, which is why Mankind goes forward as a whole. In totality, you all represent the mass consciousness of every soul and you have been carefully nursed and led through your experiences in the roles you have chosen to play." — SaLuSa, channeled by Mike Quinsey

The Choice Between Duality and Ascension

by SaLuSa, channeled by Mike Quinsey

The ascension finish line is in sight, but you will have had to enter the race if you are to cross that line. Even so, there are still hurdles to cope with and we encourage and help everyone to complete the course. In reality, you all commenced many lives ago, knowing that this wonderful opportunity would be presented to you all before the end time. As you know by now, right up to the last it will be your choice as to whether you ascend. When the stirring starts to occur within, you will wonder what is happening in your life, as you will know that something is missing. It is likely to be an unsettling time, until you realize that the answers are also within. You will find that you are awakening to the urge to find your true self. You will know that you are more than just your physical body, and feel your spiritual awakening opening your eyes and heart. Sooner or later your path will open up, and the way will be lit with the truth.

The question is, "Do you want to remain in duality, or break out of your sleepwalk and move fully aware into the Light?" What awaits you is largely beyond your present understanding, but as you rise up, so your consciousness will expand. So many beings accompany you on your journey, and they will do everything in their power to help you and urge you ever onwards. You will surely know that, if you are one such soul, you are well on the way to the completion of your experiences in duality. It will be clear to you that you have learned your lessons and are ready to move on. There may be some tidying up to do on the way home, but a smooth pathway will carry you to ascension.

Life seems to be a series of unconnected events, but in fact they are all connected, which is why Mankind goes forward as a whole. In totality, you all represent the mass consciousness of every soul and you have been carefully nursed and led through your experiences in the roles you have chosen to play. It has been planned very carefully so as to awaken you slowly but surely, in a gradual rise in consciousness that you could cope with. The powerful energies coming to you from the higher dimensions have paved the way to the future, and will soon see you through the next big step in the process of ascension. No attempts to prevent it will succeed, and it matters little what shall precede it on Earth. Just keep your sight on the reason you are here at this wondrous time, and know that any difficulties will be short-lived. It is the end result that is important, which comes with the closing of the cycle of duality.

Are you feeling a bit disconnected from day-to-day happenings, because you will in some ways become distant as you move more into a different mindset. Be assured you are not losing your memories, but the mundane events of Earth no longer have the power to hold your attention. Your mind is often "somewhere else" and you temporarily lose touch with reality. Your consciousness is moving into a higher vibration, as you merge closer to your Higher Self. You are in strange times, compared to what you normally experience, but as the veil is lifted, the Light will illuminate your mind with the truth of who you really are. In reality you are great Beings of Light, who stepped down into the lower realms for no other reason than that you wanted to expand your evolutionary experiences.

Dear Ones, there is so much to take in during these changing times, so let go of the old ways unless they serve the Light, and be ready to change your beliefs to those that come with the New Age. The way is simple and the direction is sign-posted by Love and Light. If you can find balance and harmony in your life now, we would say that you are already living from a higher state of consciousness. Is it then no wonder that you feel different to many people around you, and find their ways no longer acceptable? It is a sign of the separation that is occurring at the present time, and it is a perfectly normal development.

Once we can have direct contact with you, the changes will speed up and people will gravitate to those who are like themselves. Groups with a common interest will grow, and their contribution to the work ahead will hasten the whole process. This is something we encourage, and be assured we already know who has the abilities or qualifications to assist us. You will be invited to share our technological knowledge, and help use advanced equipment to clean up your Earth. It will not take long by your standards, and then all efforts can be concentrated on restoring your rights. The gap between where you are now and where you need to be must be bridged as soon as possible, to smoothly transition you to the ascended state.

If you are unclear as to what it all means, it will be spelled out once we can use your media to reach you. The immensity of what is to come will astound you, and certainly the speed at which it will take place. Life for many will change to become a happy experience and full of excitement, as you are lifted up out of your suffering and your needs catered to at last. We speak of both your material and spiritual needs, as each is important to lift you up. Your fairytale ending to life is to move into your new reality, and it will be befitting for humankind, who have gone through so much heartache and disappointment. Happiness and joy will be the key to your next challenge, as you leave duality for good.

We of the Galactic Federation will close this message by assuring you that everything is moving forward satisfactorily, despite outer appearances. Naturally, we would have preferred that matters were more advanced, but we have to go with the flow. We ask you to do the same and adjust as necessary, because the obstacles will be removed and the way forward will become a smooth journey. Make allowances for the strange times you are in, which are unlike any previous occasion and result from conditions imposed upon you by the dark forces. They never intended that you should be settled and have time to enjoy your lives. That approach will however be consigned to the past very soon, and replaced with all that is needed for a happy life.

I am SaLuSa from Sirius, and most pleased with your response to our presence, which makes our tasks so much easier to carry out.

Thank you SaLuSa.

— Mike Quinsey

(The above is the message SaLuSa gave to Mike Quinsey on May 31, 2010.)

"The Mayan calendar ends at December 21, 2012. That is a fact. However, the reason it stops there is open to speculation ... The other writings of the Maya have been interpreted to indicate that this particular date is a transition period for humankind. However, transition does not mean destruction and death; it simply means change." — The Librarians, channeled through Rev. Rhonda Smith, Ph.D.

The Dream of Unconditional Love

by The Librarians, channeled through Rev. Rhonda Smith, Ph.D.

Far too many people have their knickers in a twist about the date of December 21, 2012. And in fact there has been a great deal of propaganda about that date. But it is just a date, even though people do tend to listen to and believe such propaganda. So why is this propaganda created at all? Because there are those who believe that power OVER is what the world is about, and they have used this type of propaganda to forward their "control" for a very, very long time. This propaganda of fear, if it can be caused to exist in the general populace, will blind individuals to what is really happening. So, instead of falling into fear, let us examine what that date really is and where it came from.

The first thing to realize is that the Mayan calendar, which so many are saying indicates the end of the world in destruction on December 21, 2012, is actually several calendars created from much earlier calendars. The Mayan calendar is a system of calendars and almanacs used in the Mayan civilization of pre-Columbian Mesoamerica. These calendars had been in common use through the region as far back as the 6th century B.C.

For example, the Mayans employed aspects from the earlier calendars of the Zapotec and Olmec, as well as the contemporary Mixtec and Aztec. Therefore, the Maya calendar is actually the result of several calendars that the Mayans "tweaked" by creating extensions and refinements, as well as blending them, which resulted in the most sophisticated calendars of the period. The only reason that it has taken on "importance" is because, even though there are calendars pre-dating it such as the Egyptian, the Mayan calendar and the Aztec calendar have been the best-documented and the most understood, until fairly recently. As you know, when you do this kind of tweaking, it is a lot like the old game of "telephone," where you start with one thing and when you get to the end it's completely different.

The Mayan calendar ends at December 21, 2012. That is a fact. However, the reason it stops there is open to speculation. It is quite possible that the work on the calendar stopped simply because the Maya died out and no one continued the work! The other writings of the Maya have been interpreted to indicate that this particular date is a transition period for humankind. However, transition does not mean destruction and death;

it simply means change. Of course, those who are afraid of change may interpret that to be death and destruction. Remember, that does not make them right! Also remember that the only thing that is permanent in this reality is that everything is constantly changing. That is how we all grow and evolve.

Another thing to examine is that the Mayan calendar is based on sun cycles. December 21, 2012, is the end of a grand cycle. It coincides with our sun's alignment with the Central Sun of our galaxy. That is also where several other "time lines" converge. All these energies coming together indicate that there will be a great energetic shift in consciousness, a new vision of who we are and a deeper understanding of the concept of how "everything is conscious and connected." The awareness of that concept will indeed change everything. It will change people's perspectives and their beliefs, which will inevitably change the world. This is not something to fear, but rather something to celebrate.

Since the Mayan calendar was based on other calendars, one has to wonder where those other calendars came from and what they were based on. As everyone knows, if you want the truth of the matter — any matter — you keep looking back until you find the source. There has been a discovery of a calendar — also carved in stone — within the Great Pyramid. This calendar dates back to 2560 B.C. It has been decoded and it does show the transition at December 21, 2012. However, it goes on and shows another transition at 2030 and another transition in 2057. The thing that is really wonderful about this is that it took humanity millennia to get to this point of transition in 2012, and once that first step is taken, it only takes us 18 years for the next step and another 27 to the last step into maturity as a group. Well done!

In actuality, one thing becomes very obvious. If the "root" calendar (for lack of a better term) continues past December 21, 2012, we are not going to blow ourselves up on that date! In fact, the Great Pyramid calendar continues well past 2900!

Let us turn to another ancient modality: numerology. Records indicate that numerology began with the Sumerians and their mathematics around 3000–2300 B.C. The Babylonians built on this and the Chaldeans, an area of Babylon, expanded upon it around 600 B.C. During the time of the Mayan calendar, the Chaldeans were setting up a system of connections between the vibration of mathematics and the human condition: Chaldean numerology.

It is interesting that the Babylonian mathematics of 2000–1531 B.C.

and 1531–600 B.C. — the fall of Babylon and Chaldea — are consistent and continuous. The Greeks and other Hellenistic cultures drew heavily on this knowledge. They probably gained access to it through the conquests of Alexander the Great. Alexander ordered his people to translate the astrological information and so the knowledge continued on, both for astrology and numerology.

The vibration for December 21, 2012, is a vibration of initiation into Spirit in the physical. The vibration for a day within a month within a year is a combination of all those vibrations. Starting with the year which underlies all 365 days, you have 2012 which is a 23/5 in the group consciousness level. This is the fullness of YOUR personal spirit approaching the changes and achieving true freedom of choice along with everyone else's.

The month is 12/3, which is an integrated person, primarily from the physical perspective, in balance and manifesting who they are through their choices by approaching everything from the "physically knowing" perspective.

The day is 21/3 which is an integrated person, primarily from the Spirit perspective, in balance and manifesting whom they are through their choices by approaching everything from the "Spirit knowing" perspective.

The combination of these vibrations indicate that everyone in the group consciousness will have the potential to see "the whole picture" and make their choices from that knowledge. In short, everyone has reached the top of Maslow's pyramid of self-actualization in their physical lives. This is definitely a transition point for humankind!

The totality of the vibration for December 21, 2012, is 29/11. This is the vibration of initiation. It is balance in Spirit (20) through learning all about the physical (9) and moving into experiencing being a true, complete human being which is Spirit in a body suit having a physical experience (11). This is a new adventure, a new dream. The Mesoamericans believe we are dreaming what we think is real. Unfortunately, looking at human history, we have chosen to dream a nightmare. If we choose to fear this date, we surrender ourselves to those who want to take our power rather than embracing our truth. Now it is time to dream the real dream of joy, unconditional love and wisdom which is our inheritance. It is time, so dream unconditional love!

(The Librarians, through Rev Rhonda Smith, Ph.D.
      www.theawakeningcenter.com and www.theawakenet.org)

"… as the sun prepares to unwind 11,500 years worth of internalized energy, there's also an unwinding of the human experience. We've attempted to make life appear linear and separate from all of God's other creatures. Now, a new vision is beginning to appear." — *Hunt Henion*

What Will Happen as Our World Unwinds

by Hunt Henion

Due to the pull of the planets for the last 11,500 years, the magnetic field of the Sun has been winding up around itself to a breaking point, in a way that has manifested in the last few years as a conspicuous absence of sun spots. Low sunspot activity translates into a cooling influence, which counteracts our warming core and the greenhouse effect from our increasing emissions. Some professional observers worry that the sun may be "sick," because they figure we should be seeing more sunspots as evidence that the sun is entering the next solar maximum cycle on schedule. However, this unusual exterior coolness could very well be part of the natural cycle designed to balance the earth's increasingly hotter interior during the end of this 11,500 year cycle, as the sun prepares to unwind its magnetic fields and eject all that stored up energy.

"Every 11,500 years...the Earth's magnetic field reverses, and the earth starts spinning the other way." — Patrick Geryl, author of The Orion Prophecy

Meanwhile, as the sun prepares to unwind 11,500 years worth of internalized energy, there's also an unwinding of the human experience. We've attempted to make life appear linear and separate from all of God's other creatures. Now, a new vision is beginning to appear. Soon, our sun will throw off its magnetic field, disrupting the Earth's magnetism in the process. This will trigger the unwinding of our carefully constructed illusions, and remove technological power from the hands of those who control it for their own purposes.

Since the beginning of human history, we have twisted the universal laws of unity, lowering our vibrations on many occasions, so we could more easily see things the way we wanted to see them. Yet, the more we've tried to iron out reality onto our 3D linear plane, the more we have actually twisted natural reality (God's reality)! That was our right, and it served a purpose. However, our vibrations are rising again now, and the reality we've all come to know is beginning to unwind.

We're beginning to see the unity of all things and our connection with others more clearly. Events are beginning to catalyze this process for many. By the sun throwing off its magnetic field, it may cause a profound quiet (and panic by others) here on Earth. It's possible that all of our magnetic media will be erased. So, sun activity could very well be the next big step in this catalyzing process.

The big question everyone wants to ask is "What else will happen?"

The answer that's important for everyone to understand is "Only what needs to happen!"

What we each need is different. Personally, I really believe the changes around 2012 will come to be known as the pivotal time when everyone created the life they wanted. We may be making different choices, but all of our vibrations are rising. Everyone will be maturing quickly in the days ahead, and our guidance will be getting stronger and clearer all the time.

As for the specific dangers and miracles that lie ahead, the Hopi have said that the land under those who are in harmony with Mother Earth will "rise like plateaus." Edgar Cayce has said that people will influence their immediate environment so that their surroundings will respond to their needs. Many seemingly miraculous things will be noticed in the coming years as we all quickly outgrow the belief that things happen for random reasons in a chaotic universe.

For those who want to know what exactly will happen, we were told in channeling several times now that "Planet X" will fly by about the same time as we experience a 180-degree magnetic pole reversal and about a 20-degree crustal shift. Perhaps Planet X will be the catalyst for the polar shift. However, this prediction of magnetic and crustal shift (which I originally reported in my best-selling book, *Looking, Seeing and Knowing*) coincides closely with Drunvalo's recent relaying of the living Mayan authorities' prediction. They predict the same 180-degree magnetic pole reversal and a 16-degree (versus our 20 degree) crustal shift.

We were also told in channeling that although it's not likely, a black void of about 25–30 hours may accompany this shift, (also tentatively confirming the Mayan prediction as relayed by Drunvalo). We're also told that the future Earth changes will probably play out pretty much the way Gordon Michael Scallion describes. Rasha has confirmed that although Scallion has missed on many of his more recent predictions, his future map of the world is very accurate. (You can find it online.)

Still, everyone's experience is going to be a little different. We're all learning to accommodate our multidimensional selves and integrate our many dimensions into this physical world. So, our experiences are going to be increasingly multifaceted. We're also going to have more access to our higher nature and abilities. Trust them!

(Excerpted from *The Renewal: A Synopsis of Possible 2012 Changes*, by Hunt Henion, www.shiftawareness.com)

Learning to Cooperate with the Transformation

"That small voice inside of you is encouraging you to now listen to your inner wisdom, to explore other possible realities, to discover the many ways in which the Divine is offering assistance and support." — Elizabeth J. Foley

Awakening the Lightworker Within

by Elizabeth J. Foley

Finally our long-awaited awakening is here. Isn't it wonderful, magnificent, exhilarating, and at the same time scary, frustrating and confusing? Just HOW are we supposed to do all this "evolving" in the midst of our busy daily lives? What in Heaven's name does the Universe want from us? How would we know if we are Lightworkers? And oh, before we consider awakening the Lightworker within, what does that word even mean?

These are but some of the many questions that went through my own thoughts and the thoughts of virtually every one I've met along my spiritual path. At one point or another, we find ourselves questioning our Divine purpose: "Is there more to life than just a 9–5 job?"

We become curious about the "what else" of life. I believe that the moment we ask this question is the moment of our personal awakening!

Many that I see in my spiritual practice and in workshops had intense experiences leading them to begin their quest. Mine, like so many others, did not come with a big bang. It was a gradual shift and I am grateful for it. Either way, the real question is, "Where to from here?" No matter what triggers this awakening, what we do next is what matters most.

So who or what *is* a Lightworker?? A Lightworker is simply one who agreed on a soul level to help make a difference here on Earth. In essence, we are all Lightworkers, here to learn from and teach each other, and to care for the planet! When we make a conscious and sincere commitment to doing this, the Universe uses whatever method we are open to as a means of communicating with us.

That small voice inside of you is encouraging you to now listen to your inner wisdom, to explore other possible realities, to discover the many ways in which the Divine is offering assistance and support. Life as we know it is ending, a new era is beginning and your own soul is triggering changes within you. These changes, whether subtle or dramatic, are unique to each individual. From a deep stirring of the soul to psychic awakening, or perhaps the feeling of being overwhelmed even to the point of insanity. Some feel like the rug was just pulled out from underneath them. Others experience intense energy running through their body and their chakras being fully activated.

Your soul is the director and orchestrator of this experience. Become more mindful of your inner voice, and awareness expands naturally.

This is the key, for spiritual awakening can take you on an intriguing journey, one that shows how the Divine within can guide and totally transform an ordinary person. I moved from corporate America, working in the bio-tech and pharmaceutical industry to now devoting my life purpose path to my own spirituality and to awakening others to their spiritual power and mastery.

Simple everyday happenings lead to intriguing spiritual discoveries and you see synchronicities occurring all around you. It may even feel like magic. You may be reading this very chapter right now because a series of synchronistic events led you here.

Maybe, lately, you have become curious about metaphysics and your own spiritual path. Like me, you might have picked up a deck of oracle or tarot cards and found the results fascinating, and now you want to take your knowledge to the next level. Nothing happens by accident.

Awakening often begins with or causes the questioning of long-held beliefs. Some identify this process as a "Dark Night of the Soul." My own "night" seemed to last for *decades*. Yet, when you choose to reach deep inside, a whole new world is shown to you. Spiritual awakening sparks a new energy inside of you that can help you to understand the bittersweet lessons of life. I learned — and I promise that you can too — to see parents, friends and loved ones with different eyes, and recognize just how their connection with you is the perfect opportunity for soul growth.

Then there are those inexplicable events, like a sudden clear intuition, vision, visitation, healing or something more subtle but clearly outside the realm of the ordinary. We are surrounded by energy and at times we can fully and intimately experience that energy in a variety of ways.

My book, *Awakening the Lightworker Within*, is filled with accounts of experiences and encounters with angels, archangels, Ascended Masters, nature spirits and other spiritual beings. At first I doubted these experiences, or thought they were just sheer luck. Then I finally realized and accepted that another world coexisted with my view of reality. The Universe truly supports our journey and will provide validation; we have only to ask and then keep our hearts open for the response!

There is no amount of education that can prepare an individual for the 2012 awakening. Many are experiencing new feelings that go beyond logic and reason. Some are drawn to work with the angelic realm, as I do, while others are guided to do healing and energy work. As a former counselor, I have noticed many psychotherapists and other health professionals seeking ways to interweave spirituality into their clinical work.

There are so many ways to interact with positive Divine energies, and for many, the messengers — often called angels — are among the purest, easiest and most loving ways to connect. Regardless of age, religious background, or the nature of a challenge, I have found that people are delighted to discover the presence of their angels, as well as the ease of conversing with them! Your angelic team is giving you signs that they are encouraging you to advance in your spiritual development and your knowledge of them and yourself. The angels say that soon the blind will see and the deaf will begin to hear, for humanity is awakening from its spiritual slumber. As the veil becomes thinner, the illusion of separateness (which prevents us from remembering who we truly are) is dissolving.

The awakening certainly challenges us to consider other possibilities and to see ourselves and our life through different eyes. Know that we are not, nor have we ever been, alone! Our own soul prompts us to use our innate spiritual faculties, so that we hear, see, feel and know that Spirit is around us. It is never too late to awaken to following the compass of your soul. My very first chapter shares with you the details of just one of the times I have been blessed to support and witness a beautiful transformation. In this case it was a person in her late 60s with terminal cancer who found healing, peace and comfort in the arms of the angels while making her transition home.

It is a time of remembering how the Divine works in very loving, mystical and fun — yes, fun! — ways. By working from your heart center, you can learn to recognize the loving nudges of spirit. Some may call this taking a leap of faith, or learning to face your fear. Whatever words you use, ultimately you learn to rely on the hand of God to guide you.

Everyday challenges will suddenly serve to bring you closer to your mastery and to find greater purpose in life. To paraphrase the question Lee Carroll asks in the foreword of my book, "What if reading *Awakening the Lightworker Within* helps you to accomplish all of this more quickly than I did?" I can assure you that the energy of these times is definitely more supportive than the older energy!

Your spiritual contract is creating a metamorphosis and a leap of spiritual consciousness that Earth has not seen in eons. It is the transfiguration of the soul ... it is a Divine Awakening!

Now, as ever, it is your personal soul decision to awaken or not! You are invited to create your own shift of consciousness. It is time to celebrate your life and your Divine Awakening. It is time to awaken the Lightworker within and enjoy your journey.

Your spirit is calling, how do you answer?

(Elizabeth J. Foley, Reiki Master, International Angelologist and author of *Awakening the Lightworker Within*, *Angel Readings for Beginners* and *A Guidebook for Advanced Angel Readings*.

www.divinehealing.us and www.angelstreetpublishing.net)

Take a Leap into 2012 — and Beyond!

by Barbara Schiffman and Camille Leon

Is December 21, 2012 just a date on the calendar for you — or is it a personal invitation from the Universe to encourage you to evolve?

Regardless of what occurs in the world and/or within our collective consciousness in 2012, start preparing for it now by fully experiencing life as an adventure. Strengthen your ability to flow with paradigm shifts of any magnitude by consciously taking "Leaps of Faith" so you can expand from the inside out and outside in.

According to sci-fi/fantasy author H.P. Lovecraft, "The oldest and strongest emotion of mankind is fear, and the oldest and strongest kind of fear is fear of the unknown." Most of us fear what we have not yet personally experienced, even if it's something we desire.

When something challenges us, adrenaline is automatically released in our bodies to give us energy to either flee or fight any threats to our survival. This biochemical rush also creates emotions like anxiety and fear. When we can't run or fight back — or don't need to — we often freeze. In fact, some people get so overwhelmed by the feelings triggered by changes, challenges or opportunities they become emotionally frozen most of their lives.

We experience what doctors now call Chronic Stress when our inner adrenaline regulators get stuck in the "on" position from overuse. This common condition of contemporary life depletes our emotional, mental and physical reserves. It can also squelch our sense of childlike wonder as well as our desire for adventures and new experiences. In response to stress, many people narrow their focus and start experiencing the world primarily through an increasing array of electronic gadgets rather than face-to-face and moment-by-moment.

By encountering life "up-close and personal" through actively stretching your own Comfort Zone, you'll gain more strength to handle paradigm shifts wherever and whenever they occur in your life and the world-at-large.

As life breakthrough coaches, we've both learned first-hand that it's easier to leap into the unknown when you have plentiful reserves of courage to draw upon. These can be built by taking small leaps today as practice for taking bigger leaps later. This works the same way as lifting five-pound dumbbells helps athletes begin strengthening their muscles until they can heft fifty-pound weights with ease.

Courage is spontaneously gained by transforming the unknown into something that's personal and familiar. Through building courage this way, you also reap the rewards of what we call The Exhilaration Effect: the adrenaline-endorphin rush that propels you more deeply inward and more powerfully forward in every aspect of life.

The positive aftershocks of taking a leap literally rejuvenate your brain and clear your mind by forging new synapses. This feeling of exhilaration also silences negative emotions and thoughts, which can feel disconcerting. Most people are accustomed to the familiar sensations of fear and doubt that are constantly stimulated by media and advertising messages, as well as the comments of our fearful friends and relatives. As you begin viewing the world through fresh eyes and experience yourself as confident and capable, however, you'll discover there's a wider range of options available than before. As your mind and heart open, fear evaporates and faith takes over.

How can the Exhilaration Effect help you move through 2012 shifts? Taking Leaps of Faith replenishes your Courage Reserves, which will help you respond effectively to challenges and opportunities instead of reacting automatically and resisting them.

What do we mean by a Leap of Faith? It's that initial step toward a goal which seems far away or even impossible to reach. It's doing something you didn't think you could do — being something you didn't think you could be, saying something you didn't think you could say — and being transformed at the cellular level by the expansion that ripples throughout your life.

According to Wikipedia, taking Leaps of Faith in any part of life requires "believing or accepting something intangible or unprovable, without empirical evidence." Naturalist-author Henry David Thoreau noted "we must walk consciously only part way toward our goal, and then leap in the dark to our success."

For some people, a Leap of Faith might be speaking up for themselves to an authority figure at work or a domineering relative. For others, it could be letting go of addictive behaviors or self-destructive thought patterns. It can be quitting a job that's been draining your energy for years to start a new business or artistic endeavor that may not be instantly profitable but makes your heart sing. For many of us, it's stepping into our own spotlight after years of hiding in life's shadows.

One quick and easy way to enhance mental, emotional and spiritual courage is by doing a series of simple things you've never done before, like driving a different route to work or cooking a new dish. These may sound like easy tasks, but breaking out of old routines and trying something new often provokes high anxiety, especially in people who don't feel secure.

After successfully accomplishing a variety of unfamiliar tasks by choice, it's much easier to try larger and less predictable leaps. In the process, don't be surprised to discover that some actions which at first feel stressful or scary are actually fun. As composer Virgil Thomson suggests, "Try a thing you haven't done three times. Once, to get over the fear of doing it. Twice, to learn how to do it. And a third time to figure out whether you like it or not."

The first time you do something new, notice how you move through The Exhilaration Effect's Six Stages of Leaps of Faith: **Expecting**, **Exploring**, **Experiencing**, **Examining**, **Extrapolating** and **Expanding**. Whether the leap calls you forth or you're thrust into its path against your will, you're likely to feel resistant at first. When it won't go away, you can begin exploring what's required to survive it and even thrive!

Finally, you'll step bravely into the unknown and "just do it." After the shock — and adrenaline rush — of the leap wears off, you'll realize you're safe on the other side. We suggest you pause and catch your breath before you reflect on what you did and how you did it. This helps you re-calibrate so you can do more of it now that it's familiar (even if it's still not easy).

The courage of taking a leap, no matter what it is, will expand your capacity to experience Life no matter what occurs around you. You'll also gain fresh perspectives on aspects of your life that were not apparent to you before. You may also notice the world treats you differently as your energy, behavior, communications and desires expand. These are all part of the positive paradigm shifts that will re-calibrate your post-2012 world.

We predict that the wisdom gained from experiencing new things and the exhilaration of doing them (and not just thinking about them) will generate "a new you" more attuned to the energy of 2012 and beyond. But please don't wait until 2012 to get started — begin now!

(Barbara Schiffman and Camille Leon, co-creators/co-authors of *The Exhilaration Effect: Building the Courage to Take Your Leap of Faith*, coach people to have more fulfilling lives by taking leaps of faith.
www.ExhilarationEffect.com, email: ExhilarationEffect@live.com)

"You are the divine embodiment of Mother/Father God, expressing yourself as these creative Master Beings and co-creators to the Company of Heaven. We are creating this reality, sweet ones, with you." — The Elders, channeled by Anrita Melchizedek

An Understanding of the Cosmic Rays

The Elders (ancient, celestial beings and High Council Members of the Order of Melchizedek), channeled by Anrita Melchizedek

Welcome, sweet ones. It gives us great pleasure to be with you as you experience the energy of the Cosmic rays through the related Co-Creative Councils of Twelve, for the Cosmic rays take you dimensionally through the higher dimensions into the Cosmic Heart and Mind of Mother/Father God. At this Now moment, the reality exists for you to truly step into your multi-dimensional nature as Master Beings and Keepers of Light to this earth plane in this wonderful Golden Age of Light. Further to this, the anchoring and activating of these Cosmic rays are assisting all of life on this earth plane to experience a higher light quotient through the amplification of these Divine energies of Illumination and Light.

Now how are the Cosmic rays in particular assisting in this planetary ascension, and how are they connected to 2012?

Well, all the rays come forth from the Cosmic Heart of Mother/Father God, and the six Cosmic rays in particular are stepped down to this earth plane dimensionally — coming through from the fourth dimension, the fifth dimension, the sixth dimension, the seventh, the eight and the ninth dimension, respectively. Each of these ray vibrations brings through stellar codes of light, sonic vibrations, qualities, colors and the overlighting of core groups of Light Beings. The Cosmic rays are not only assisting in activating the dormant DNA, but are assisting in building the I AM Avatar blueprint. Many of you are stepping forward into this role, in what we are call the first wave Souls in human embodiment of the I AM Avatar Blueprint, choosing to merge and integrate the energy of their I AM Presence, choosing to be the World Leaders, Teachers and Wayshowers in this Now. For as you shift energetically into these new fifth-dimensional encodings of Light, you take on this mantle of leadership in order to assist others to move through these gateways of Light into the higher-dimensional frequencies of Light.

In terms of how the rays have been affecting you individually, sweet ones, you may have experienced an acceleration of the ascension frequencies, parallel mergers, past life memories, all merging in this Now, to take you to another level of Cosmic Consciousness awareness: You will further be developing your Ascended Master skills, so to speak, of enhanced telepathy, clairsentience, clairaudience, clairvoyance — it matters not — as well as finding the ability to more easily transcend the dualities on this earth plane — in other words, being able to view through your master eyes and hold yourself steadfast in this Light.

As these Cosmic rays travel through this quadrant of the galaxy and into this solar system, onto the planets within this solar system and then onto earth, they move into Shamballa and then into the Christ Consciousness Grid, the Unity Grid within and around this earth plane, and from there into the sacred sites and ley lines. Key codes are then activated and available initially for the Light Workers on this earth plane; and as we continue to assist in building the ashrams to these six Cosmic rays (which will be complete by the year 2012/2013), the Cosmic rays will be available for all of life.

Experiencing the energetic vibrations of these higher rays accelerates the embodiment of your magnificent Mighty I AM Presence. For these fine light vibrational frequencies take you into a level of Cosmic Consciousness awareness to experiencing the Illumination of the Higher Mind, the Wisdom of Mother/Father God, and the energy of unconditional Love. Now this is being experienced in pockets or waves within and around this earth plane, and bringing your focus to the Unity Grid of Light is one of the best ways to experience the amplification of these Cosmic rays, which are currently being activated to the maximum Cosmic Law will allow through these Divine Dispensations of Light being given to the earth plane at these accelerated times of Cosmic Consciousness awareness. As these gateways and portals of Light are being activated on this earth plane, they further allow these gateways out of this earth plane, and the ring-pass-nots existing around this earth plane and around this solar system to be shifted to a level where you take yourself beyond these boundaries, beyond these ring-pass-nots, into the next level of Light.

All of life, sweet ones, is being lifted into the Heart of Mother/Father God. This is the ultimate journey and is being experienced energetically at this Now moment. Through the energy of the rays, all of life has the ability to step into Unity Consciousness and the experience of coming home. For through the amplification of these Cosmic rays, you are creating this bridge of Light back into the Cosmic Heart of Mother/Father God and lifting yourself in Cosmic Consciousness awareness from dimension to dimension. And as the Ascended Master skills deepen, so you will have the ability to start to translate the time and space continuum and experience different dimensions and realities through these dimensional frequencies from On High. We look forward to this, sweet ones, as you collapse this time/space continuum into this ever-present now, experiencing all realities of Light in this Now moment.

As these first-wave I AM Avatar humans, building this etheric electronic body of Light — this perfect Adam Kadmon blueprint — know that we are watching you in delight and in awe. For you are proving that you are capable of truly wrapping yourselves in these garments of Light, of truly stepping into your roles as these Keepers of Light, Spiritual Leaders and Wayshowers. You are truly coming together as these galactic star-nations of Light, sweet ones. You will find your strength and understanding through joining not only these legions of Light from On High, but forming this on earth as you are embraced in the energy of Mother Earth and connected through this Unity Grid of Light, this Christ Consciousness Grid of Light holding this crystalline structure and the highest potential of all life on this earth plane.

You are the divine embodiment of Mother/Father God, expressing yourself as these creative Master Beings and co-creators to the Company of Heaven. We are creating this reality, sweet ones, with you. This journey has already occurred, and yet — in this timeline — is still occurring. We embrace you with such Love as we see you stepping into these garments of Light, as these Avatar Light Beings, merging completely with your Higher Light, as your Higher Self of the Light and Christed Overself of the Light, or Mighty I AM presence. And we look forward to this journey with you into this Golden Age of Unity Consciousness and Love.

(The Cosmic Rays were activated initially in the summer of 2010 by a joint initiative between Children of the Sun Foundation and The Melchizedek and Pleiadian Light Network and thousands of Lightworkers around the globe. For invocations to individual rays, please view our You Tube Channel at http://www.youtube.com/user/AnritaMelchizedek. For more on the Twelve Rays and Six Cosmic Rays, please view the articles section on our website and related e-Books at www.pleiadianlight.net.)

"Energetically, see yourself riding the big one. Notice how you keep your knees bent, your body aligned, and you are able to maintain balance as you coast over wave after wave. If you wipe out, you see yourself getting up from the surf with a big, goofy grin on your face as you climb back on to your board and ride, baby, ride. This is what the Big Shift is all about — riding the waves."— Adele Ryan McDowell, Ph.D.

Packing Your Cosmic Backpack for the Big Shift

by Adele Ryan McDowell, Ph.D.

The world is changing at breakneck speed, as we inch ourselves closer and closer to the planetary shifts of consciousness and being. And, as with any new birth, there will be some pain, contractions, doubt, fear, and maybe even a bit of panic, as we work to bring forth a bouncing new world that operates from a place of co-operation versus competition, understands the interconnectedness of all and honors the Earth and all sentient beings.

Like the tectonic plates shifting on the Earth's crust, these shifts will change our *terra firma*. What we call "ground" will shift into a new gestalt. We will be in a state of flux — which for many of us is rather uncomfortable. We like what we know; we gather comfort from the familiar. We human beings, for the most part, are change-adverse. Change is scary: we often keep the devil-we-know in a stranglehold, rather than deal with the new and unknown behind door number one.

Change on a grand scale, like these planetary shifts, can be unsettling; we may find ourselves uncertain, afraid and out of balance. We may feel unglued, untethered and (most likely) very stressed.

Stress and fear can bring out the best and worst in us. Often we feel better prepared and more in control when we plan ahead. With that in mind, here is a suggested Big Shift "packing list" for your cosmic backpack:

A sense of humor

This is a must. It helps keep everything in perspective, is a terrific stress reliever and keeps you in the here and now. And it always lightens the load and creates bridges for connection.

An open hand

No need for white-knuckled or tight-fingered control; leave that management style at home. Being stoic and appearing stonily strong do not make your fears or insecurities disappear. Those tightly-coiled worries remain compacted inside of you, fueled by your runway brain, and ready to collide and explode into the next brick wall you encounter. It serves no purpose in these days of expanded thinking.

In lieu of the tight-fisted approach, allow your hand to be open — open to receive, open to share, and open to allow. These types of fluid exchanges will help you negotiate the Big Shift with greater ease.

Flexible feet

Flexible feet offer you motion and mobility so that you can receive new operating instructions. This flexibility allows you to jump and leap, twist and bound as you leap to the next level of consciousness.

Surfing skills

Energetically, see yourself riding the big one. Notice how you keep your knees bent, your body aligned, and you are able to maintain balance as you coast over wave after wave. If you wipe out, you see yourself getting up from the surf with a big, goofy grin on your face as you climb back on to your board and ride, baby, ride. This is what the Big Shift is all about — riding the waves.

Linking cords

The planetary shift is all about oneness: the interconnectedness of all. To aid and abet the process of connection, it is most helpful to consciously bring these energetic cords to help you join with others, one by one, like twinkling lights on a strand that will encircle the globe we call home. Kindergarten had it right: it's always easier with a buddy or two.

Mother Earth's phone number

Speaking of home, bring your connection to the Great Mother Earth with you. With this connection, you can find solace, wonder and healing symbols. The Mother will hold and ground your energies and offer you comfort and peace.

Third eye

During the Big Shift, you will be called on to be your Best Self, and that requires you to learn to trust yourself — more specifically, to trust your many forms of intelligence, your instincts and your intuition. You know and absorb and realize far more than you think you do. Trust yourself. It is one of the most important steps on the rung of the ladder of personal transformation.

Answers to two questions

With this planetary birth of consciousness, there will be change afoot on every level. With this consideration in mind, it is helpful to determine your unique responses to these two questions:

What makes you feel safe?

Perhaps it's being in nature, surrounded by others, a deep connection to someone special or trust in the invisible realms. Or maybe it is room to breathe, space to run, time to be, or togetherness with others? Identify those qualities — and there will be more than one, idiosyncratic to you — that provide you with comfort and allow you to feel safe.

What makes you feel sane?

Each of us has a number of grounding elements that make us feel less scattered and out of control — in other words, sane. These are personal coping responses to the cumulative effects of daily stress. These elements are drawn from our personal repertoire to help us emotionally and mentally reboot. Some examples might be creating order, making beauty, being understood, having choices, discretionary time, a place to clear your head, a heartfelt conversation, and the like.

Take some time and discern those elements that provide you with the ability to maintain your mental and emotional equilibrium and keep yourself sane.

Mirror

The mirror allows you to really see yourself. It permits you to look deep into your soul and remember who you are — and to remember that you raised your soul's hand to be here — at this moment, at this time — for this very shift. Your unique skills, perceptions, talents, passions, joys, experiences, light and love have already been programmed into the mix to make this Big Shift — this journey of consciousness — a grand adventure. Allow your magnificence to unfold.

One heart with stretch marks

And last, but never least, bring along your heart that has been squashed-upon so many times that of all the judgment and cruelty has been pounded out. This heart is held together with stretch marks from moments when you were cracked wide open, again and again, so that your heart could expand and hold greater and greater buckets of compassion, understanding, forgiveness and unconditional love.

If you can only fit one thing in your cosmic backpack, make it your big, squashy, stretch-marked heart. It is the perfect accompaniment for the Big Shift.

Take precious care, dear ones. I look forward to waving hello as I see you ride the waves, tread the paths, and dance in the light, as we shift, shift, shift, all together now.

(Adele Ryan McDowell is a transpersonal psychologist and higher consciousness teacher and the author of *Balancing Act: Reflections, Meditations and Coping Strategies for Today's Fast-Paced Whirl* and *Help! It's Dark in Here* (2011). You can find more at www.theheraldedpenguin.com.)

Growing Up God

by Linda Martella-Whitsett

My son Adrian had missed his curfew again. Again I lay awake in bed, imploring God to protect him from his youthful inanity. Praying for Adrian's safety, I asked outright for divine intervention. I prayed this way frequently, because my son's teenage ventures afforded me lots of experience with motherly worry.

A few years later, I would pray more earnestly. At nineteen, Adrian had enlisted in the U.S. Marine Corps and was deployed to Iraq with the first-in troops toward the end of 2002. I entered into a daily prayer vigil. I was with my son in Iraq, in my heart, wrapping him in a cloak of protection. In the words of Unity's late poet laureate James Dillet Freeman, I proclaimed, "Wherever you are, God is!" Insisting no time or distance can separate us from divine love, I held my son close in my awareness. Moreover, I imagined my son sheltering a shaking comrade and soothing a terrified rookie. I cast my thoughts well into the future, picturing there a man of integrity and purposefulness serving the world.

What had been happening within my consciousness during those years that my way of praying changed so dramatically? I know. God was growing up.

God is growing up, as human consciousness is rising to reclaim our divine identity. In the past, claiming Divine Identity would get us excommunicated, or publicly vilified. We would be considered blasphemous and egotistical. We would be consigned to the mass identification of ourselves as "children of God." As I grew up and grew spiritually, I wondered, must I always remain a child of God or shall I grow up to *be* God one day?

When I was a child, I spoke like a child, I thought like a child, I reasoned like a child; when I became an adult, I put an end to childish ways (1 Corinthians 13:11).

In countless ways over countless eras, spiritual masters have attempted to convince us that our nature is divine and we may identify ourselves as divine:

Every being has the Buddha Nature. This is the self.

(Mahaparinirvana Sutra 214)

That which is the finest essence — this whole world has that as its soul.
That is Reality. That is the Self. That art thou.
                                                        (Chandogya Upanishad 6.8.7)

I say, "You are gods, children of the Most High, all of you."
                                                                (Psalms 82:6)

For God to grow up, or more palatably, for us to assume our Divine Identity, nothing less than a revolution, a reformation of our prayer life, must occur. We must shift from asking to declaring, from pleading to affirming, from expecting intervention to imagining possibilities, and from addressing God to *being* God. Isn't it time for us to stop begging and start being?

According to Abraham-Hicks, asking is natural to us. Asking is not a function of language. Asking occurs as we feel the inner movement of heart's desire. As we identify our heart's desire, we are connecting with the Divine capacities that bring our desire into expression — Divine Love, Divine Wisdom, Divine Strength, Divine Imagination, and all the Divine powers. We shift the focus of our words from *asking* to *declaring*. I stopped asking God to protect Adrian and began declaring my son's eternal, absolute safety and security.

Similarly, we must stop pleading for a desirable outcome. Instead of imploring God-out-there, we affirm the greatest absolute truth revealed in the moment. I stopped placing my good and my son's good out into the future: "We'll be okay when he returns safely." I realized Divine Love *is*, which means Divine Love cannot divide us by circumstances or dissolve our unity by any means. *I* grew up as I realized whether my son died on the battlefield or returned home with limbs intact, the love between us would always be.

Just as adolescents move away from expecting our parents to solve our problems, we too must stop expecting God-out-there to intervene on our behalf, as if God could. Realizing God is not a superhuman but the intelligence underlying all, we mature in our prayer life as we assume our Divine Identity. In my own way I did this, imagining the good my son was doing and the good that was possible for him in the future.

Eventually, as we grow up God, we stop addressing God altogether and begin *being* God. Being God meant for me to adopt a divine perspective, to look upon my life and my son's life from the broadest view. In order to be God in this experience, I had to stop acting like an only-human with only-human worries. I was called upon to *be* God, which I understood was to stand strong in my circumstance, sure of the absolute truth above all circumstance.

Now is the time for God to Grow Up

The "Me" generation grew up in the 1980s. Everyone was in therapy and a twelve-step program. We were healing the personal sense of self — getting over ourselves! Our prayer was to "let go and let God." I refer to this time as the decade of *purge*.

The nineties gave rise to the Internet and instantaneous mass communications. The information age drew our attention toward greater knowing. Television shows such as *Touched By an Angel* and *Buffy the Vampire Slayer* banked on our obsession with seeing the invisible. We prayed to identify with the divine. I call the nineties the decade of *surge*.

The first ten years of the new millennium brought reality TV, Facebook, and blogs. The world became flat and our neighborhood became the world. We believed we could have it all and studied The Law of Attraction as a means to getting it all. Our prayers became demands upon the universe to give us what we wanted. 2000 to 2010 I label the decade of *splurge*.

We have purged our personal demons, awakened to our spiritual nature in the surge of the nineties, and experienced our inner power to create during the splurge of recent years. God is growing up and now we are socially conscious, interested in the good of all, desiring to live in unity and harmony. Now is the era of the *merge*, when God becomes a grown-up. We are no longer begging God but *being* God. God is declaring profound intention. God is affirming absolute truth. God is imagining possibilities. God is being God.

(Rev. Linda Martella-Whitsett is an ordained Unity minister at Unity Church of San Antonio. Linda's upcoming book, *Stop Talking to God: Prayer and Meditation for the Evolving Soul*, is one of four finalists in The Next Top Spiritual Author competition.

Visit www.nextopauthor.com or find Linda at www.unityofsa.org.)

"When you discover that you want to experience a greater depth in life than the apparent external things you see and acquire, you take your first steps on the spiritual path. You embark on a journey of new beginnings, self-realizations and miracles in your life. All things in your life begin anew." — *Tracy Latz, M.D. and Marion Ross, Ph.D.*

"Psychosis" Versus Awakening Intuition

by Tracy Latz, M.D. and Marion Ross, Ph.D.

"Am I going crazy?"

What do you tell someone who reports hearing voices inside their head, or someone who talks about seeing visions of people or spiritual beings? In many cultures, this is not considered normal. Sometimes, it is more accepted as a cultural belief if it is described as a visit from a deceased family member during a time of grief or acute stress. The idea of a spirit guide being called upon for counseling or advice is also accepted in some cultures (e.g. Joan of Arc's "voices"). Children who speak about such things are usually believed to have an overly developed sense of imagination. While many highly creative people, inventors and geniuses have expressed hearing voices that are the source of their creativity, most people who report hearing voices are labeled as just being "crazy."

Physicians, psychiatrists, psychologists and other mental health professionals have historically been trained that people are delusional or psychotic if they report seeing or hearing things that other people do not see or hear. A hallucination is defined as a profound distortion in a person's perception of reality, typically accompanied by a powerful sense of reality. It may be a sensory experience in which a person can see, hear, smell, taste, or feel something that is not there. Hallucinations are often described in truly serious psychotic disorders that need to be medically treated, such as schizophrenia, psychotic depression, severe mania, schizoaffective disorder, certain seizure or tumor-related disorders of the brain, and illicit substance-induced hallucinosis. Hallucinations are also frequently described in dissociative disorders and anxiety disorders such as post-traumatic stress disorder. (Disclaimer: It is important to note that a person on medication for treatment of psychiatric disorders or under the care of a physician not discontinue or adjust dose of medication without first consulting their treating physician.)

"Extrasensory perception" is a phrase that was introduced in 1940 by Dr. J. B. Rhine of the Department of Parapsychology at Duke University. It is used as a general term to describe all sorts of phenomena that cannot be perceived through our physical senses. This includes clairvoyance (seeing things beyond the range of our normal vision) and clairaudience (hearing things beyond the range of our normal hearing). These perceptions may not only be from beyond the range of our normal, physical senses, but also from different times or from regions that are not on the physical plane. The Institute of Noetic Sciences has continuing research about intuition, the effects of our consciousness and intuition on the physical world, and the role of intuition and consciousness in health and healing.

"Why would anyone want to hear voices or see things that aren't there in physical reality? I don't want people to think I'm crazy!"

In fact, many people throughout history have actively pursued activities to open up their intuitive or spiritual senses by choosing to train in ancient mystery schools, enter monasteries, sit in meditation in ashrams, or make pilgrimages to connect with the energy of natural sacred sites. It is fueled by an inner calling to connect with your True Essence — who you truly are. When you discover that you want to experience a greater depth in life than the apparent external things you see and acquire, you take your first steps on the spiritual path. You embark on a journey of new beginnings, self-realizations and miracles in your life. All things in your life begin anew. New hope, restored faith and a deep sense of love begin to fill your life through your spiritual studies. As you discover the power of your heart, love sets the tone of each day. You are now here on Earth with a deeper understanding of your life and a greater sense of your spiritual purpose for being here. You no longer feel alone. There is a sense of belonging and a kinship with all life.

"Okay... so what if I DO want to develop my intuition and expand my abilities? How do I do that?"

In order to access our inner senses, inner wisdom or intuition, it is important to understand that we *all* have inner senses or intuitive capabilities. However, we may each experience our intuition in different ways. Some will tend to use clairsentience ("clear feeling"), where they will just "know " the answer or feel it in their "gut" or in their "heart." Others will use clairvoyance ("clear vision"), where they will receive an intuitive message through a vision, symbol or an image in their mind. And yet others may experience their inner sense as clairaudience ("clear hearing"), where they hear the answer as if by telepathy (this is not a hallucination). With practice, a person can easily develop access to many types of inner senses, including those of smell, hearing tones instead of words, being able to get information by holding an object, and various combinations of these different methods. It is much the same as building up a muscle at the gym. The more you exercise it, the more powerful it becomes and the easier it is to make use of it.

Going within through various forms of meditation, attaining a quiet prayerful state, sitting quietly in nature, or being in the energy of a natural sacred site are some of the best means to cultivate your inner space and to access your inner "still small voice." We also can gain immediate access to our intuition in a busy, wakeful state whenever we are present in our heart with great compassion or concern for a friend or a loved one. Have you ever noticed how easy it is to receive intuitive information when you are getting it for someone else?! It is easier to get into our heart or to have compassion for someone else than it is to do so for ourselves.

What keeps us from getting into our heart to receive intuitive messages for ourselves? We are limited in our ability to connect when-ever we experience a sense of unworthiness (feeling unloved, guilty, ashamed), abandonment, anger or resentment, heartache, inadequacy or powerlessness, fear of the unknown, stress, or when we lose sight of who we really are. Once we remove these barriers (we give guided meditations as well as rapid tools and techniques to assist in our books *Shift: 12 Keys to Shift Your Life* and *Shift: A Woman's Guide to Transformation*), it is important to establish new habits of heartfelt connectedness so that you can rapidly tap into the Universal Wisdom that lies within each of us.

Practice is the best means to initially "open your third eye" and stretch your natural intuitive abilities or inner senses. Pick a daily time that works best for you to spend even just 10 minutes or as long as 45 minutes to quiet your mind and be aware of the stillness within. Do not concern yourself with what you think you "ought" to experience; just let whatever happens to occur. Your most developed type of inner sense will likely be what you notice first. For instance, if you tend to be more clairvoyant, you will likely "see" symbols or colors or other visual images; you might even see whole visual scenes as if you were watching a movie. If you are more clairaudient, you might begin to hear an inner voice stating a phrase, a conversation or discussion, music or sounds of nature. However, if you tend to be more clairsentient, you will likely just "sense" that you are in a certain place or "sense" a certain color, rather than seeing it or hearing anything. In my experience teaching meditation courses, the clairsentient people most often report frustration early on in meditative practice because they often feel like they are "doing something wrong," since they do not "see" or "hear" anything. We cannot emphasize enough that there is no wrong way to meditate. Each person has their own unique experience. You can meditate with eyes closed (what I recommend for most beginners), eyes open, sitting still, walking, or doing simple repetitive chores.

Acquaint yourself with that teacher within you. It knows who you are, where you have been, where you are going, and what your gifts and abilities are. You are truly brilliant. Be still and know that "I Am."

(Tracy Latz, M.D. (practicing board-certified integrative psychiatrist) and Marion Ross, Ph.D. (transpersonal psychologist) are known as "The Shift Doctors." They are metaphysicians, keynote speakers, holistic healers, co-authors of 2 meditation CDs and the books *Shift: 12 Keys to Shift Your Life* and *Shift: A Woman's Guide to Transformation*," and can be found at www.shiftyourlife.com.)

Preparing for the New Earth

by Dolores Cannon

As the New Earth is formed, when you first cross over, you will be in your physical body. Eventually over time it will turn into a light body, just the way these other beings are.

My subjects are being told that they must change their diet in order to make the adjustment into the new world. You have to be lighter. Heavy foods will hold you to the old Earth. They have said many times that the ideal foods are live foods: fresh fruits and vegetables. Lighter foods will allow you to change your vibration and the frequency more easily. They say to stay away from sugar, and to drink lots and lots of water — the true value of water is unfathomable.

Many people have asked, "What am I supposed to be doing?" We are here to help each other, be there for each other. There are two things that we have to get rid of in order to go to the New Earth: negative karma and fear. There is good karma and negative karma. As long as you are bogged down with negative karma, you are going to remain on the old Earth, because the way the law of karma is set up, you must repay it. Too many people are caught up in negative karma and do not know how to release it. That is the reason why new souls had to come, because they don't have karma, and they can help others to release theirs. You have had many lifetimes with the same people, revisiting the same circumstances and not resolving them. Until you can stop that cycle and get off of the wheel of karma, you are not going to be able to evolve upward.

The way to get rid of negative karma is to forgive and let go. Some of my clients have said, "I can't forgive them. You don't know what they did to me!" That is what makes people sick: holding on to this baggage and garbage and not letting it go. You have to let it go because it is not hurting the other person, it is only hurting you. The first thing you're going to have to do is forgive. Now, sometimes that is difficult to do face-to-face with the person. And sometimes the person with whom you have negative karma has died. You don't have to face the person to ask for forgiveness and to forgive them; you can do it mentally. Picture the person in your mind and just speak to him or her mentally.

Focus on the person and send your forgiveness and love. Everything comes back to love.

It all goes back to your treating others as you would want to be treated yourself. It begins to turn to the vibration of love and that is the most powerful thing there is.

Now, the second thing you have to do after that is to forgive yourself, which is also very difficult. People are always good at blaming others without looking at themselves. It takes two to create a situation. Even though you consider yourself to be the victim, you're still a part of the whole thing, perhaps even from a previous lifetime. You have to look deep inside to be able to see and accept your part in the circumstances, and then forgive yourself. Release it and let it go. It has no place in your life any more.

The second most important thing they say you have to do if you want to go to the New Earth is let go of fear. Fear is a paralyzing emotion. It's the strongest emotion a human has. If you don't understand something, you are going to be afraid of it. Fear drags you down and holds you back. If you have love there is no fear, but many people live their entire lives in fear. There is so much on TV, in movies, and elsewhere trying to generate fear. You have to think for yourself and ask lots of questions. Make up your own mind.

Then what you come up with will be your truth. Most of the time what we fear never happens anyway. Fear is so powerful that when you think of something over and over again, through the law of attraction you draw that very thing toward you. You have to get rid of fear because it is debilitating and binding; it will hold you to the old Earth.

Meditation is very helpful. They say the best time to meditate is just before the sun comes up, when all the Earth is quiet and still. However, any time that you can set aside for yourself to be quiet, alone, and just relax will be beneficial. Then ask your questions and listen for your answers.

At a recent conference I attended, Annie Kirkwood, author of *Mary's Message to the World*, described a vision she had of this transformation. She saw the Earth sphere begin to pull apart, like a cell when it divides in two, and then it separated into two Earths. And on the New Earth she heard them saying, "We did it, we did it!" On the old Earth she heard them saying, "Poor thing, she died believing all that." One group is not even going to be aware that anything has happened.

I would like to end with a quotation from my book, *Convoluted Universe, Book Three*, a message given during a session with one of the souls who have come directly from God:

"You are God. It is given to you to manifest your God-beingness. Open your God self, and allow the light to enter. From within will come such light. It will manifest from the very core of your being. The world which you envision is already inside of you. You are not moving to another planet. You are breaking out of your shell. This planet — this shell — is bringing forth that light."

It is given to you to enter your light fully — fully and to draw it out. And to say, I AM LIGHT. Nothing in God's beingness can exist without the permission of God. I say to you, YOU ARE GODS. YOU ARE THE LIGHT!

(Dolores Cannon is a past-life regressionist and hypnotherapist who has specialized in past-life therapy since 1979. She is the author of fifteen books and has done over 1000 radio appearances. She travels all over the world teaching her unique technique of hypnosis and bringing the message of the coming New Earth.

This article was compiled from an interview with Dolores Cannon by *Light of Consciousness*, as well as her DVD, *Awaken*, from a November 2009 lecture in Long Beach, CA, and her books *The Convoluted Universe, Books Two Three*.

For further information, visit www.ozarkmt.com.)

" ... we, humanity, will greatly assist this time in our history and the history of Mother Earth by remembering our 'creating nature.' The Angelic Realm, as they watch and support us, realize that most of us have forgotten what magnificent creating beings we are." — Barbara Joye

Remembering Our Creating Nature

by Barbara Joye

As I work with the Angelic Realm and am a conduit for them to share messages with the world, the one message that they continue to share, over and over again, is that we, humanity, will greatly assist this time in our history and the history of Mother Earth by remembering our "creating nature." The Angelic Realm, as they watch and support us, realize that most of us have forgotten what magnificent creating beings we are.

With this realization, they requested that I bring forth (as a co-author with The Angelic Realm) the book *The Creating Formula: Achieving the Life You Deserve,* as a way to assist us each in remembering and returning to our creating nature.

In this writing, The Angelic Realm shares what they call "The Creating Formula." The formula, however simple or complex you choose to perceive it, speaks to all aspects of life and all ways of living. It is, quite simply, a remembering of the elements of creating, of the beliefs that best support the optimization of those elements, and of the manner in which the elements interact.

In its simplest format, The Creating Formula is:

$$C = \{(Ec \times Fp \times LoA)/DT\} \times Ai3.$$

Within this formula is the interaction of all of the energy of the cosmos, the physical frequency of each creating individual, the utility of the Law of Attraction, the impact of Divine Timing and a full explanation of such, as well as the necessity of action — instinctual, intuitive and intended.

This formula explains how each of the elements interacts with the others. Further, the formula explains the energetic manner in which the elements interact and process in the physical body. Embracing of this formula is necessary for each individual to create their optimum life. This supports an easier and more dynamic evolution through The Great Transition — the 2012 Paradigm Shift.

Within this formula are also the beliefs to hold as a creating being. It is the perception of the Angelic Realm that humanity has forgotten or forsaken many of the beliefs that, at a soul level, each individual understands and with which they are innately aligned. In the view of the Angelic Realm, humanity (each of us) has shifted away from these beliefs because the beliefs were too difficult to hold while we attempted to remain in alignment with the societal norm. In other words, the Angelic Realm perceives that we (each of us) have chosen the societal norms over our own soul's knowing — our own connect with the heavens, the Angelic Realm, and The Divine/The All.

For this reason, the Angelic Realm would like to assist in our remembering by sharing the beliefs that we have forgotten. Through this sharing, it is hoped that we each will begin our remembering process; a process so necessary for easing the challenge inherent in The Great Transition.

The beliefs to remember and to incorporate into The Creating Formula include:

- You are a Soul in a Physical Body — align first to your soul;
- You are a Soul with an Agenda — listen as your Soul Team assists you in remembering your agenda;
- You are More than Sufficient for Your Agenda — know this and live in the knowing;
- Creating in the Physical is a Process of Collaboration and Alignment — you are not intended to be a sole creator. Create in community;
- Creating in the Physical is a Process of Honoring — honor all, including yourself and each energy you interact with in your creating;
- You are a Soul connected to a Soul Team — you are not alone in your creating. You are simply the member of the team capable of creating in the physical;
- You are Creating that which is Not Known — release the expectation that you know what you are creating. In releasing, you are able to create more dynamically and expansively;
- You are the Bridge between the Non-physical and the Physical — that is your role and the combined role and interactive dance of your soul and mental ego;
- You are Responsible to Align Your Soul, Core Ego, and Agenda — in this alignment you create the flow for the creating, you remove the blockages that currently slow or totally inhibit your creating genius;
- Creating in the Physical is a Process of Attraction and Blending — the Law of Attraction is a powerful law of the Universe and it is honored and supported in this creating process;
- Creating in the Physical is a Non-linear Process — as it is a non-knowing process. The Universe pays forward and pays back, which is different from the current Earth's expectation;

- Trusting the Universe, Trusting in Us, Trusting in The Divine/The All is Imperative — in this trusting you allow for the magnificence of the/your creating to occur;
- You are Worthy and Perfect for Your Agenda — otherwise you would not have the agenda you have. The Universe — The Divine/The All — does not set a soul up for failure on the Earth plane;
- Creating in the Physical is a Process of Allowing — and it is this allowing which seems to be most difficult for those souls in the physical to embrace;
- Creating in the Physical is a Process of Awareness — become aware, open to miracles, ignore self-created obstacles, and create.

If we each incorporate or reinforce these beliefs and perceive how the creating process is optimized, we then allow for our own shifts, which in turn support the shifting of humanity. For each individual reading this writing at this time is called to do so. For each individual reading this writing at this time is a "way-shower" and is destined to support the transition, the evolution, of humanity to the expanded paradigm introduced at the onset of 2012 and expanded during the following years.

Shift into your own knowing.

Remember and embrace the beliefs.

Accept yourself as the creating element you are.

Shift into The Great Transition — the Paradigm Shift of the Ages.

(Barbara Joye, The Shift Guru, from the book, *The Creating Formula*. www. TheShiftGuru.com.

For information on *The Creating Formula* and its accompanying *Journal of Trusting*, go to www.TheCreatingFormula.com.)

"Ascension is the attainment of spiritual knowledge, or when we become primarily light rather than dense. Our graduation into divine purity indicates we have transformed from a focus on ego or personality to functioning from our soul self, love, and humility. With the metamorphosis of ego to soul, we enhance the 2012 transition and beyond." — *Dr. Linda R. Backman*

Ego Versus Soul, Love, and Humility: Moving to 2012 and Beyond

by Dr. Linda R. Backman

Ego is both essential and non-essential all at once. If we define ego as narcissism, the blind focus on and over-valuation of the individual self, then ego could be considered highly detrimental. If we use the term "ego strength" to refer to a capacity to maintain emotional and mental equilibrium throughout most of the minor and major storms of life, then ego is a priceless faculty to possess. When it provides internal equilibrium along with an egalitarian view of all people, we come to honor the ego in everyone.

The expression "Soul Self" refers to love in the most wholesome sense of the word. At its highest point, love is as indescribable and inexpressible as the Divine, its ultimate Source. And like the Divine, it can only be accessed through emotion and non-linear experience.

Consider the polarity between the forces of ego and love, and what lies between. The beauty and intention of regression hypnosis is that the client receives spiritual input from a non ego-based source. Mysticism and the ascension experience speak to the communion with our Soul Self while embodied — grasping the awareness that we are pure light at our core.

Embodiment is the height of divine task — a sacrifice, even — as our soul must confine itself in coming to live for a time within a container that grounds it to the frequency and density of the planetary laboratory. As a soul, we are compelled by an innate need to return to incarnation, lifetime after lifetime, in order to reach the height of spiritual wisdom. Ascension is the attainment of spiritual knowledge, or when we become primarily light rather than dense. Our graduation into divine purity indicates we have transformed from a focus on ego or personality to functioning from our Soul Self, love, and humility. With the metamorphosis of ego to soul, we enhance the 2012 transition and beyond.

In body, holding fast to the awareness of our true or divine self can be a struggle. The paradox is that we are thrust into corporeal life precisely in order to advance as souls. We need to recognize human ego as a complex and tenacious mask covering the perfect beauty of the soul, and to strip away the camouflage of our human "warts." In sum, we need to become simultaneously aware of both ego and love to reach the "summit" and discover our true self.

Eli: Finding Oneness

"There is a sense of gossamer as I move through the spiritual realm. I am being told that there is more love coming into the world. We will feel it in every cell of our bodies, but it is not the love that we know in our earthly selves. It is not even an emotion. It is completeness. It is simple understanding.

"The whole of our human society is about materialism and incompleteness. Now we stand in the gap. We know what needs to be brought in. We must hold on to Spirit and to the place or person that we are. We can then transmit the completeness.

"Our collective beliefs are evolving. We are all trying to find our way home. This is where we do the changing. Let this key open the door of your heart. Let your bird out to fly. Look into your heart. You know the answer, too. Having the separateness of incarnation compels us to work our way back to oneness. We must feel the paradox of separation in order to find our way back and feel the completeness of that oneness."

Lila: On Ego and Evolution

"A message from your Wise Council: Your soul evolution has allowed you to reach a high level in soul standing. Those like you who can put aside ego and serve as a conduit of universal light are usually humble and shy. Such souls do not judge. They have understanding and wisdom, and infinite compassion for each soul. Those with great ego on the other hand, who need to be recognized and do not honor their deep spiritual privilege, will have their privilege taken back. The laws of the universe must be learned."

Eli and Lila offer a rich depiction of the dichotomy of ego vs. soul. Eli's Spiritual team mentions "standing in the gap." When consciously unaware of ourselves as a Soul Self, we are mired in the bog of materialism. Discarnate, we are wholesome waves of light and energy as a soul.

During between-lives soul regression, the "gap" is seen as an inability to merge our corporeal existence and our pure spiritual being. The "bird" that can take flight from within our heart is the inexplicable but palpable love of the Soul Self. Joining body with Spirit is the key to releasing the energy of higher self. When this union is experienced and exhibited, it creates a fulfillment previously unknown to the being in incarnation.

Lila offers a number of powerfully descriptive words such as humble, evolution, high, ego, light, shy, judgment, compassion, conduit and privilege.

To distinguish "love" from "ego," simply remove the terms ego and judgment and see what remains.

Judgment stems from ego. As our soul evolves, we begin to operate more and more from a perspective of light. This in turn leads to the privilege of serving as a conduit for love, and so we are likely to exhibit compassion and be humble, and perhaps even a little shy. Lila's message reminds us however that we can also lose the privilege of being an advanced soul.

Sandra: Going For It

Sandra is a highly experienced soul who was not required to reincarnate. Her Soul Color is purple. She chose to come in order to be a powerful support and advocate for others, but she has initially had to struggle to find inner joy.

Sandra's spirit guide tells her:

"You can be as big as you want to be now.

"The woman who is embodied as your teacher in this lifetime could not handle the competition from you. Human competition is a human problem, and in your life as a performer, you have already discovered that competition must be set aside. It does not make for a more accomplished performance.

"Performers must go beyond. You know what you need to do. Go out and be happy."

Competition stems from ego. To believe in our own capabilities regardless of anyone else's skills appears to be the message from Sandra's spirit guide.

When we are following our passion, trusting that we are competent, we accede to a place where we have the ability to operate from our core truth, our Soul Self. Ego is not truth. It is a mask to hide our human frailty. Our guides and teachers endeavor, moment by moment, to direct us toward healing that which is incomplete or inauthentic within us and stepping into the greater purity of our Soul Self.

Love is the energy of Spirit, the energy of the soul. The words love, spirit, soul, and the Divine are interchangeable. Functioning from our ego is not operating out of love for others or ourselves. Ego attempts to camouflage our human fears and concerns, and thereby entrenches them. At our nucleus, however, we are nothing less than love, the highest level of Spirit.

Our only task in each lifetime is to recognize and come to realize who we truly are. We are a soul residing in a body and having an incarnation, not the other way round. We are pure love that has traveled to Earth, arriving in this dense, Earth-based laboratory. We are charged by our spiritual team to experience life moment by moment in order that our pure, loving Soul Self might advance on its journey. We are souls that are here to progress.

When we shine our loving heart, our Soul Self, out to others, some will receive it gracefully, while others will stay mired in ego and illusion and not have the wherewithal to perceive it. It is not our job to force anyone to accept our love. Everyone opens up to love at their own rate.

The more we continue to radiate love unconditionally, the sooner souls trapped in their illusory egos can begin to let go of their hardened human shells and start to soften their hearts.

As we progress in our soul journey, we achieve greater ease, ability and likelihood of functioning from the soul level rather than out of ego or human personality. Imagine a ladder in your mind or the stairs in your house. There is no hierarchy, no "better or worse." Just like everyone else, we begin our soul's journey toward soul progress on the ground floor.

(Dr. Linda R. Backman is a licensed psychologist and regression therapist who wrote *Bringing Your Soul to Light: Healing through Past Lives and The Time Between* (Llewellyn Worldwide Publishers, 2009), from which this article is an excerpt. www.RavenHeartCenter.com)

Using Emotional Technology to Jump Timelines

by Cat Thompson

The current definition of Emotional Intelligence says: "Emotional intelligence (EI) describes the ability, capacity, skill or, in the case of the trait EI model, a self-perceived ability to identify, assess, and control the emotions of one's self, of others, and of groups."

Emotion is a fourth-dimensional experience. To know the truth of this, think about something that happened in your past that is still able to trigger intense feelings. Emotions are not bound by time or space. We can feel them years later as intensely as when they originally occurred. This means the ability to travel through time and space lies in the feeling body. And, as we all know, our feelings cannot be manipulated, controlled or forced into feeling a certain way. The idea of controlling our emotions, or controlling others' emotions, sets up a structure which can never understand the true nature of emotional power. Emotions are magnetic in nature. Therefore, what we feel strongly is what we attract. Yet, if we cannot avoid specific emotions, how do we stay out of fear, mistrust, anger and hopelessness?

In most indigenous peoples who still practice Shamanism, there exist technologies that go far beyond our western, scientific understanding — that do, in fact, appear as true magic. I believe that authentic emotional intelligence is the ability to manipulate reality — to draw something into 3D manifestation, or to jump timelines. EI can be seen as the marriage between Shamanism and Quantum Mechanics. The transformational teachings in our culture now realize that we create our reality. Understanding how emotion is utilized in these teachings is the key to accessing our super-powers.

The singularity we are approaching in 2012 can be seen as a cluster of possible realities and timelines, all converging together. Most of us can feel the chaos of this: every day there are so many different stores to grab our attention. Where shall we invest our belief? What story is actually true? How can we possible believe we are going to come out of this safely and joyfully if the news each day is so dire?

Here is some simple advice for how to navigate the chaos ahead. First, where do you want to end up? What world do you choose to live in? What does it look like? How does the economy work? What role does government have in this world? How do people balance personal ownership and shared resources? In other words, how does the world you land in actually work?

Then use your tools of visualization and manifestation to insure you actually get to that world. Build a vision board, or a photo book, showing what your world looks like. Get specific and detailed. If you're living in an intentional community, how is the work done? Who owns the water, the air, the darkness, and the silence? What does "work" mean? What kind of a job will you have? The more specific you can be, the more firmly you will be grounded in that world. (I recommend playing Sim City, as it quickly teaches how governments are designed to work.) The more people who can share your vision, the faster you can all attract the future you desire. Rather than wasting any energy on reacting to what you don't like, use all your energy to create a bridge to the world you choose. Instead of networking meetings, have visualization meetings, and get yourself and your community working out the details of your next life.

Then, as things become more chaotic (because, after all, that is what happens when we hit a timeline/reality knot), use your vision to hold yourself steady through the rapids. If you feel fear arising, know that fear simply tells you, "I don't know what is coming." Breathe, bringing yourself into the moment, and show fear your vision. "We're going here," you can tell fear, "so hang on and believe. We are safe and supported." When you feel victimized, or disempowered, write it all down in a journal and then breathe and move on. (Writing down intense feelings locks them into a time/space, freeing your emotional energy). Acknowledge your feelings, listen to what they have to say, and use your vision boards to stay anchored into a future of joy.

Above all, believe that we are approaching one of the most amazing opportunities of the human race — the ability to jump timelines — and if we want to have the most excellent ride of our lives, we need to be prepared. The more you know about the world you are planning to jump into, the easier it will be to recognize when that world appears on your doorstep. The more excited you feel about this new world, the faster you pull it towards you. The more you allow your feelings to flow through you without judgment, the faster they transform to power.

Turn off the news. Compost the newspaper. Focus on your own life, your own community, and the world you most desire to inhabit. Then use your magical skills to build a bridge to that world, and when it bumps up against you, JUMP!

In loving service, Cat Thompson

(Cat Thompson is a pioneer in the field of emotional intelligence. Visit her website www.emotionaltechnologies.com for a cornucopia of tasty offerings!)

"...always come from a place of love. ... Feel love; feel and know Nature better. Feel simple, and simply feel gratitude for the beauty of the developing new order." — Hunt Henion

How to Prepare for Ascension

by Hunt Henion

Here is a five-step program to help you shift your awareness, so you can be better aware of The Shift and stay in harmony with it:

1. Spend as much time as possible outside. Try to relate to all you see in Nature and all you know that's below the surface. Declare yourself part of it. When we're inside, our own creations take over our consciousness. These inside involvements and creations may comprise our individual path in life. However, they need to be put in to perspective if we hope to secure our niche in Nature, as she lightens her load in preparation for ascension.

2. Avoid opinions and judgments. We all want things to be as easy and comfortable as possible, and we all think we know how that should happen. However, Mother Earth is running this show, and she has her own agenda. Trust the unseen order and know that Mother knows best. Work on detachment from preferences, especially from self-indulgent activities. Rest is a priority that Nature understands, but when we're expected to give up our plans, we need to give them up freely, trusting the Earth and the Universe to provide all that's really necessary.

Also, try to see life from the viewpoint of the family, friends and foes around you. Those who are cemented into one viewpoint won't be prepared to offer the love and understanding to others which a unity consciousness demands. Nor will they be prepared to let go of their known world and accept the coming massive changes.

3. Simplify. Spend time and attention on those with whom you feel the strongest bonds. Simplify your thoughts about these people — forget their faults and focus on the love. Simplify your activities, spending all the time you can with those you love and doing things which bring you closer to the Earth. Eat simpler. Be simpler.

4. Gratitude. If the only prayer you said in your whole life was, "Thank you," that would suffice. — Meister Eckart

Gratitude can make you happy and flexible and, incidentally, help you catch the ascension bus when it comes along. Work on cultivating a feeling of constant gratitude for the infinite blessings of Nature, no matter what is happening in your outer life. Express this gratitude whenever possible, and hold all complaints until your silence extinguishes them.

5. Expect to be the person you've always wanted to be. Just as we prepare to give up our personal comforts and preferences, we need to give up all we think we know about our limitations. The whole world is changing, and we ARE changing with it.

Now go back to Number One and review the program. Promise yourself and Mother Nature to spend at least a little time outside each day, where you'll surrender your priorities to her higher purpose. While you're out there, re-examine your commitments with a focus on your bond to your loved ones and Mother Earth. Let your attention to those things in life that belittle you fall away as you gather around yourself the simple things which really matter.

Feel gratitude and express thanks in every way you can for your ability to stand in Nature and to stand in your truth. Know that this is who you are as an individual and as part of the ascending Earth. Let love and gratitude fill your thoughts and feelings.

Our channelled answer for a busy world where remembering even five steps may be too difficult, was to "Live in the heart chakra," (the heart of the heart) and always "come from a place of love."

What we feel is what we are. Feel love; feel and know Nature better. Feel simple, and simply feel gratitude for the beauty of the developing new order.

(Excerpted from the best-selling book, *Looking, Seeing & Knowing* by Hunt Henion, www.shiftawareness.com)

Restructuring our World

"It is only natural that every soul desires to be loved, and if you first love yourself, it will be easier to express love where others are concerned. See in yourself and others the godself that you all are, and release all judgment. You will find that life suddenly feels different, and that a peace enters it that knows no equal. Live and let be all that is around you, and bless all those souls sharing your journey with you." — *SaLuSa, channeled by Mike Quinsey*

The Power of Thought

by SaLuSa, channeled by Mike Quinsey

Never forget the power of thought, it can heal you as an individual and collectively determine your future. So no matter what appears on the horizon, you can decide how it will manifest in your lives. The coming changes that are going to uplift you will be welcome, but there are also others involving physical changes to the Earth. Depending on where you live, they may have little effect — if any — upon you, and in addition our presence will ensure that they are directed in such a way, to avoid maximum damage. Whatever happens around you, your visualization to introduce a harmonious and balancing energy will help to lessen the effect. Also bear in mind that outside help, such as ours, is more readily available when your prayers or supplications are received. For example, it is only in recent times that you have made a powerful call for help from us, and that has given us permission to respond. Without such a plea it would otherwise have been seen as interfering with your freewill.

On Earth you have draconian laws that are often neither fair or justified, and are, in fact, introduced purely to keep a firm control over everything you do. You are also subject to the same Universal Laws as we are, and unless they are observed, even higher powers will intervene. It has happened many times before where your civilization is concerned, resulting in meetings and councils to decide the right course of action. Wise souls adjudicate on such occasions and we observe and obey their conclusions. Man tends to be hasty and does not yet consider the effect of his actions upon others. Wars are, for example, the ways of those who have no understanding of the oneness of All That Is. They not only incur immense negative karma, but set your evolution back very severely. The wanton killing of innocent people as a means to settle your differences is a gross insult to your Creator. You have absolutely no right to take the life of another soul, and the fact that such abominations occur is an indication of how corrupted some of you are. However, we are pleased to say that as the Love and Light has spread around the Earth, so the sanctity and preciousness of life is becoming understood.

Realize that as you travel the path to ascension, so you will raise your consciousness, and your whole concept and understanding of life will change. It is only God who can create life as you know it, and Man will never be able to ensoul his own creations. Yes, Man can create forms with limited consciousness or hybrids, but it is only a vehicle for a soul to inhabit. Can you see, Dear Ones, why you cannot "own" another soul, which is a free spirit to experience as it chooses? When two souls decide to procreate, the soul that takes their physical creation has chosen them as its parents. That is indeed a soul to be dearly loved and guided through its childhood, and allowed where possible to follow its preferred life plan. As parents have often found, a soul has a powerful urge to follow its instincts and has definite views as to where its future lies. Be proud of such a soul, and know you have been chosen because you have something of value to give each other.

Life is really not as complicated as it may appear, and if you understand Universal Laws, such as the Law of Attraction, you can do much to achieve success. Karma is often repeated because lessons are not learned, and they will continue to confront and plague you until you do. Be assured it is through this Law that you set out on your path and if you know how to use it, it will make it a lot easier. Naturally your life plan takes precedence, and your Guides will do all they can to ensure that it is fulfilled. You do not really want to repeat lessons, if you can avoid it. So often we hear you ask, "Why me?" when something unpleasant occurs in your life, but think carefully about the lesson it is bringing to you. Also bear in mind that sometimes a soul will take human form and bear the consequences to simply help another soul. We must therefore inform you again that there is no punishment involved, and God continues to love you unconditionally, regardless of what you think.

It is only natural that every soul desires to be loved, and if you first love yourself, it will be easier to express love where others are concerned. See in yourself and others the godself that you all are, and release all judgment. You will find that life suddenly feels different, and that a peace enters it that knows no equal. Live and let be all that is around you, and bless all those souls sharing your journey with you. You will be an inspiration for them, and they will begin to understand that Man is a sentient being. Duality has, as it were, thrown you to the lions, and you have fought to uphold your dignity and right to decide your own future. Hold fast to your beliefs, but be ever aware of the opportunity to take a positive step forward. Let no one force their beliefs onto you, particularly if their way is fear-based. The energy of Love is pure, comes to you from the Creator, is beyond corruption, and is all that will remain after the changes have taken place. Think upon this and do your best to follow in the footsteps of your teachers of the Truth.

As you progress nearer to ascension, you will find that the changes within yourself are becoming pronounced. You will know with certainty that you are expanding your consciousness, as would be expected of one who is following the path of Light and Love. This will be your assurance that you are well along the path to ascension, and that your physical body is becoming crystalline. In fact, it is necessary if you are to ascend with your physical body, which would otherwise be unable to exist in the higher vibrations. As you get nearer to the end times, you will get adequate guidance as to what you can do to be ready for a wonderful upliftment. It will of course be just one stage in a continuing process that will see you rising even higher into the realms of Light.

I am SaLuSa from Sirius, and when you have closer dealings with the Galactic Federation members, you will become more aware of the level that you are moving to. We really are your future selves, and in us you will see all of the qualities that are part of your Higher Self. We so often remind you that you are far more than you realize, and that lack of recognition is the result of thousands of years of servitude that has hidden your true identity. Your status has been demeaned and distorted, through the intent of the Illuminati to keep you in the dark and in ignorance. All that is changing now, and you can begin to express the real you — a loving and peaceful soul.

Thank you SaLuSa.

— Mike Quinsey

(The above message was given to Mike Quinsey on May 26, 2010.)

"Today, humanity needs our compassion and our love to go beyond all the labels of good and evil, of who's right or wrong, beyond political parties, and beyond the different races, religions and gender that still separate us. Can we find peace and balance within these differences? Yes, if we finally come to the understanding that the only borders that exist are the ones that we create in our mind."
— Martine Vallée

Making a World of Difference, One Heart at a Time

by Martine Vallée

As far as I can remember, I have always believed in the capacity that one individual has to change things. In a way, I dedicated a big part of my life doing just that through my French publishing company, Ariane Publication Inc. I have witnessed on several occasions how words can be triggers for change. For sixteen years, I made a commitment to humanity: to know and explore the path of consciousness and then to share it with my readership.

Recently, I made another commitment: to do everything in my power to turn oppression into opportunity for women and children, even if it means doing it one woman at a time. But I personally believe that humanity excels when it is fully invested in the transformation of the world, rather than in one's own personal transformation. Many times, I have witnessed what happens when several individuals are aligned in pure intention and a common quest to change things. The results are astonishing, beautiful and far more powerful than those achieved by one person.

Every single being living on this planet shares the same dream — to live with dignity, to find peace within their community, to have food when they are hungry, to have a roof overhead, to have access to education, and especially to be free of the constant fear of being killed, tortured or raped. Unfortunately, reality is quite different for millions of individuals.

Today, humanity needs our compassion and our love to go beyond all the labels of good and evil, of who's right or wrong, beyond political parties, and beyond the different races, religions and gender that still separate us. Can we find peace and balance within these differences? Yes, if we finally come to the understanding that the only borders that exist are the ones that we create in our mind.

My path is no different from yours. By that I mean that each new direction begins with an inspiration, a heartfelt surge. And when the desire to serve becomes great enough, forces in the universe line up and bring forth whatever is necessary to turn inspiration into manifestation. Inspiration is always something unique and extraordinary, since it inevitably brings about remarkable transformations. We know the exact moment when inspiration begins, but never when it ends. For that matter, can inspiration really end? Doesn't it transform into something greater?

There is a lot going on right now in the hearts and mind of humanity. Consciousness is rising, and many feel that they are at a crossroads in their life. So what is keeping us from expressing the greatest version of who we are? Fear.

I have seen over and over how fear can keep us a step back from living our potential and how ignorance keeps us from stepping into it. Fear is maybe the biggest illusion of all. It paralyzes us and blinds us to the truth of who we really are. We always seem to be afraid of something, especially of change or the future. But that is what the shift is all about: going beyond our fears to create the future that we want to see.

Our world is being transformed as we speak; it is preparing itself for the grand finale. But this transformation will not come about if the women of this world are not able to have the place that they rightly deserve. Balance has to be restored between men and women and violence stopped. When this is achieved, the world will know peace.

Women desperately need to be included in the peace processes. By nature, women are highly invested in preventing and stopping conflict, since their first motivation is the need to ensure security for their families.

In 1996, Haris Silajdzic, postwar prime minister of Bosnia, said: "If we'd had women around the table, there would have been no war; women think long and hard before they send their children out to kill other people's children."

They also have their fingers on the pulse of the community. They know what is going on at every level, and so they are very well positioned to provide essential information on what is going on in their community. Women are always the first to mobilize efforts in their communities for rebuilding and reconciliation. If their voices are heard, then lives will be changed. If women are fully recognized as part of the decision-making process, history will change. If women speak up, they enable future generations to stand tall.

I have many dreams for humanity. It is my world and I have to decide what I want to see happen, then go about and do it. And today, I'm imagining what the world would look like if half the world's leaders were women. Would poverty levels be the same or would the focus be on feeding the hungry instead of nurturing profits? If women were at the head of half of the academic institutions, would they still represent two-thirds of the world's illiterate population? I think we all know the answers to these questions.

So here we are, looking for our common destiny. I feel in my heart that compassion is the key to finding it, and that our deep sense of justice will make us stand up together and say, "This is not the world that I want to see, and I'm going to change it. Today, I'm going to make a world of difference — one heart at a time.

Martine Vallée
Montreal, Canada
        www.passioncompassion.org
        Martine@passioncompassion.org

" … the alternative to "banking education" was "problem-posing education," in which learners are encouraged to define their own problems and questions, then to draw on teachers as one resource among many for finding answers and creating solutions. This understanding of learning focuses not on information — segments of knowledge that can be deposited or dispensed in linear fashion — but instead focuses on developing within human consciousness the capacity to inquire meaningfully and fruitfully. The latter dignifies and catalyzes the human spirit." — Patricia Webb

Transforming the Human Educational Assembly Line

by Patricia Webb

Can you recall a time when you believed in your own capacity to ask purposeful questions, and to find useful answers? How far back do you have to go? Did the capacity survive in you? Or did you find, at some point in your life, it became necessary to resuscitate this essential human quality?

I stopped believing in third grade. This wasn't the first year I was barraged with the social constraints of a grade school classroom: "Sit in your seat. Listen to the teacher. Don't talk to your neighbor. No, you may not leave your seat. Follow directions. No, you may not go to the bathroom. Don't talk out of turn. Walk quietly. Stay in line."

All this was discouraging enough, but in third grade, I was simultaneously overwhelmed with another set of demands — the growing expectation of information mastery — that is, the necessity to make consistent, persuasive demonstrations of what some would call "objective knowledge."

Over the last century, across a growing proportion of the world, humanity has undertaken a momentous experiment — the mass industrialization of learning. By this I mean there has been a systematic attempt to standardize knowledge and instruction at every stage and across countless sectors of modern life. In addition, and more insidiously, human learning has also been institutionalized in keeping with the industrial model of the 20th century factory. Students — that is, people — have steadily come to be imagined as raw materials (sometimes referred to as "blank slates" or "empty vessels") that can be placed on an educational assembly line to manufacture a final product of skillful, thinking, and "productive" citizens.

Such an assessment of modern education isn't new or unique. Among those who have created similar critiques is the late Brazilian "rock star" of community education, Paulo Freire, who labeled the dominant approach as the "banking model" of education. He argued that a teacher's work has come to be conceived much like the work of stock brokers and investment bankers. Teachers are charged with making informed investments (knowledge deposits) on behalf of the larger community into the brain banks of local student populations. Schools are responsible for safeguarding those investments (retaining knowledge) and even accruing a reasonable rate of return or "interest" on the communities' investments — which are typically measured through nationally standardized tests. In this way, following a suitable period of maturation, such investments — that is, students — become available like savings bonds or stock options to enrich the community, as another crop of educated young adults enters the workplace and the world, ready to make a productive contribution to society.

Though once entered in first grade or kindergarten, this investment system or assembly line now typically has origins in preschool or even toddler daycare, and extends ever further into young adult life; no longer terminating with high school, but with technical school, college, or graduate school. Even teachers characterize themselves with astonishing acceptance as being responsible for various phases in this linear bar graph of human progress — instilling the necessary concepts and skills at each grade level to "get students ready" for the expectations and demands they'll face further along in the process.

This understanding of education is woven so thoroughly into the fabric of modern life through so much of the "developed" and "developing" world that it is rarely noticed or pointed out, much less questioned or challenged. It makes intuitive sense to most of us — it seems logical and efficient, a "no-brainer" — for it is all that most of us have seen and experienced or can remember.

The problem is that very little attention has been given to the ways in which this rational organization of teaching and learning fits, or fails to fit, with the ways people actually learn, grow, and evolve as humans with the unique quality we call "consciousness."

It's not possible in the scope of this chapter to sketch even a few of the compelling theories that describe how learning happens, in people and in communities. What's undeniable, however, is that human learning is anything but linear, orderly, or even logical. Rather, it is quirky. It's widely varied in terms of helpful methods and strategies. It is highly social — very much a function of communities. And it is often altogether unpredictable.

This is not to say that everything about education, as we know it, is unhelpful. It is simply to say that a factory or financial model of human growth and development is internally contradictory. It is therefore unsustainable, at best, and destructive to the human spirit at worst. Education that understands human learning as a series of investments intended to produce a profit, or as an assembly line intended to dispense a productive (that is, profitable) citizen, are fundamentally dehumanizing ways to understand the human spark of self-reflective awareness and curiosity we call consciousness — which is what drives learning, growth, creativity, and higher evolution itself.

For Freire, the alternative to "banking education" was "problem-posing education," in which learners are encouraged to define their own problems and questions, then to draw on teachers as one resource among many for finding answers and creating solutions. This understanding of learning focuses not on information — segments of knowledge that can be deposited or dispensed in linear fashion — but instead focuses on developing within human consciousness the capacity to inquire meaningfully and fruitfully. The latter dignifies and catalyzes the human spirit.

What needs to change in the global educational system that has become dominant over the last century is not so much the laws and regulations governing education, nor the various curricula and instructional methods used by teachers. What must be visualized, understood, and transformed is far more encompassing and more difficult to visualize than these. We need to find a more accurate and fitting metaphor to understand the nature of learning itself. This means, for starters, examining our own primary processes and purposes for learning.

This is not a problem for "the experts." Or perhaps, from another perspective, this is an area where we can all be considered experts — for we all learn every day. If we can understand deeply enough our own human capacity to ask purposeful questions and to create useful answers and paths of action, then we can begin to know about learning from the inside out. We will then be in the best possible position to create new metaphors for learning across the lifespan and across cultures and over time.

What might you imagine? Together, what might we create and transform?

(Patricia Webb is working on her doctorate, even as she contemplates abandoning the academic assembly line and devoting herself to promoting a more nurturing educational system. Patricia can be found at www.learningshire.com.)

"The so-called "new discoveries" of modern science are often only rediscoveries of secrets well known to the healers, priests and philosophers of ancient "pagan" times. Man's inhumanity to man has resulted in the loss of wisdom, records and formula: which, had they been preserved, would have solved many of the greatest problems of this civilization." — Tracy Latz, M.D., M.S, Mh.D.

The Future of Medicine and Medical Training — A Return to Holistic Hermetic Principles

by Tracy Latz, M.D., M.S, Mh.D.

According to Sir William Osler, Imhotep was the real Father of Medicine (2980 B.C.) — about 4,000 years ago. "The first figure of a physician to stand out clearly from the mists of antiquity," Imhotep diagnosed and treated over 200 diseases: 15 diseases of the abdomen, 29 of the eyes, 11 of the bladder, 10 of the rectum, and 18 of the skin, hair, nails and tongue. Imhotep treated gout, tuberculosis, appendicitis, gallstones, and arthritis. In addition to performing surgery and some dentistry, Imhotep extracted medicine from plants. He knew the position and function of the vital organs and circulation of the blood system. The *Encyclopedia Britannica* says, "The evidence afforded by Egyptian and Greek texts support the view that Imhotep's reputation was very respected in early times ... His prestige increased with the lapse of centuries and his temples in Greek times were the centers of medical teachings."

Imhotep was worshipped as a god and healer from approximately 2850 B.C. to 525 B.C., and as a full deity from 525 B.C. to 550 A.D. He lived during the Third Dynasty at the court of King Zoser in Egypt. Imhotep was a known scribe, chief lector, priest, architect, astronomer and magician (medicine and magic were used together in that era). For 3000 years, he was worshipped as a god in Greece and Rome. Early Christians worshipped him as the "Prince of Peace."

When the Egyptians crossed the Mediterranean, becoming the foundation of the Greek culture, Imhotep's teachings and philosophies were absorbed there. The Greeks equated him with Aesculapius (Hermes). He was regarded as the god of study and in later times took on some of the attributes of Thoth or Tehuti as the scribe of the gods. In the time of Imhotep, healing was considered one of the secret sciences of priestcraft. Candidates aspiring to be trained in the healing tradition underwent severe tests or initiations to prove their worthiness at various stages of their training. Among the ancients, philosophy, science and religion/spirituality were never considered as separate units — they comprised a balanced whole — and this concept was considered integral to healing modalities.

The story of Imhotep disappeared in Greek mythology over time and was forgotten for thousands of years, A legendary figure, Hippocrates, who appeared 2000 years later in the 5th century B.C., became known as the Father of Medicine. Hippocrates segregated the healing art from the other sciences of the medical training and established a precedent for the scientific separateness, incomplete healing, and materialism present in current modern-day medicine. Doctors began to be trained to only accept that which can be experienced through the concrete perceptions of the 5 primary human senses. This is why physicians today take the Hippocratic Oath.

It was the physician/alchemist Theophrastus Paracelsus (1493-1541) who wandered through Europe, Africa and Asia in search of the ancient writings and philosophies on healing and who resurrected and preserved for us the true Hermetic Principles of healing and disease. However, Paracelsus was widely ridiculed by his peers of his time as well as many physicians today. It is only a matter of almost humorous historical interest that ALL modern-day medical students are taught the Paracelsus' Hermetic Principles of Disease and Cures during a required History of Medicine class in the first semester of medical school.

The Seven Causes of Disease According to Hermetic Medicine:

1. Evil spirits. These were regarded as creatures born of degenerate actions, subsisting on the vital energies of those to whom they attached themselves.

2. A derangement of the spiritual nature and the material nature: these two, failing to coordinate, produced mental and physical subnormality (birth defects)

3. An unhealthy or abnormal mental attitude. Melancholia, morbid emotions, excess of feeling, such as passions, lusts, greed, and hates, affected the "mumia" (a disease germ unit), from which they reacted into the physical body, where they resulted in ulcers, tumors, cancers, fevers, and tuberculosis.

4. Karma, that is, the Law of Compensation, which demanded that the individual pay in full for the indiscretions and delinquencies of the past. A physician had to be very careful how he interfered with the workings of this law, lest he thwart the plan of eternal justice.

5. The motion and aspects of the heavenly bodies. The planets/stars

did not compel the sickness but rather impelled it. Hermetic philosophy taught that a strong and wise man ruled his stars/planets, but that they ruled a negative, weak person.

6. A misuse of faculty, organ, or function, such as overstraining a member or overtaxing the nerves.

7. The presence in the system of foreign substances, impurities, or obstructions. Under this heading must be considered diet, air, sunlight, and the presence of foreign bodies.

The Seven Cures for Disease According to Hermetic Medicine:

1. Spells and invocations, by which the physician ordered the evil spirit causing the disease to depart from the patient. (Of note, the Vatican recently retrained a large group of priests in the ritual of exorcism.)

2. Vibration—Disharmonies of the physical and subtle bodies (etheric, mental, emotional, spiritual) were neutralized/rebalanced by chanting spells, intoning the sacred names, playing upon musical instruments, and toning/singing. At times lights, gemstones, crystals, or cloth of various colors were placed nearby or in the sight of the sick, for the ancients recognized the principle of color and sound healing, now in the process of rediscovery. (Acupuncture, energy medicine, and energy psychology are also tools that remove disharmonic blocks in the natural flow of vitalizing energy in the physical and subtle bodies.)

3. Talismans, charms, and amulets — It was believed that the planets controlled the functions of the human body and that by making charms out of different metals they could combat the malignant influences of the various stars/planets. Thus, a person who is anemic lacks iron. Iron was believed to be under the control of Mars. Therefore, in order to bring the influence of Mars to the sufferer, around his neck was hung a talisman made of iron and bearing upon it certain secret instructions reputed to have the power of invoking the spirit of Mars.

4. Herbs and Homeopathic Remedies/Essences —- Herbs were used quite often in ancient medicine; that is where the first idea of synthesizing compounds that mimicked nature (modern medication) came from. Each herb was assigned to one of the planets. Having diagnosed the sickness by the stars (different organs in the body were linked to different planets) and its cause, the doctors then administered the herbal antidote. Paracelsus also discovered that by gathering the dew under certain configurations of the planets he obtained a fluid possessing marvelous medicinal virtue, for it had absorbed the properties of the heavenly bodies.

5. Prayer — Calling upon and allowing compassionate intercession of the Deity for the alleviation of human suffering. Paracelsus said that faith would cure all disease. Not all have strong enough faith, however.

6. Prevention — Personal responsibility for regulation of diet and daily habits of life. The individual, by avoiding the things that caused illness, remained well. The ancients believed that health was the normal state of man; disease was the result of man's disregard of the dictates of Nature.

7. "Practical medicine," consisting chiefly of bleeding, purging, and similar lines of treatment. These procedures, while useful in moderation, were dangerous in excess.

Paracelsus used all seven Hermetic methods of treatment, and even his worst enemies admitted that he accomplished results almost miraculous in nature.

The so-called "new discoveries" of modern science are often only rediscoveries of secrets well known to the healers, priests and philosophers of ancient "pagan" times. Man's inhumanity to man has resulted in the loss of wisdom, records and formula: which, had they been preserved, would have solved many of the greatest problems of this civilization. With sword and firebrand, conquerors obliterate the records of their predecessors, and then inevitably meet with an untimely fate for need of the very wisdom they have destroyed.

Modern healthcare is often symptom-focused and reactive, rather than prevention-focused and proactive. We have truly taken a separatist rather than a holistic view of medicine- separating out various medical specialties to deal with different physical body parts or systems and relegating anything that has to do with the astral (emotional/thought) body to the psychiatrists and psychologists. Spiritual issues have been relegated to spiritual advisors and the clergy of the church, temple or synagogue of the patient's choice. Patients and physicians rarely discuss nutrition, exercise, and lifestyle change, and instead focus mainly on physical diagnosis and treatment of physical disease that has already manifested. Many clinicians feel unprepared to discuss the safe and effective use of dietary supplements or herbal medicines, or how to help patients incorporate relaxation, spiritual, or mind-body practices into their lives.

Traditional Western medical school courses presently include anatomy, physiology, biochemistry, microbiology, physical examination/diagnosis, medication/therapeutic treatment of disease, and medical ethics. A holistic approach to medical training in the new era would add training in nutrition, herbal remedies, homeopathic remedies, mind-body medicine, energy medicine, energy psychology, the responsibility and power of personal choice of the patient, as well as education in the ancient wisdom of spiritual/intuitive development, astrological medicine, spiritual anatomy/ energetic subtle bodies, spiritual healing, color and sound healing, other vibrational healing modalities, soul logos, and reflective etheric healing.

In short, medical students and physicians would once again become initiates into a sacred healing path for both their self and their patients. The soul of the healer thus trained to reach a state of high vibration (with awareness of the whole person- body, mind and spirit) would then connect with the soul of the patient who had a true desire to return to or maintain a state of vibrant health. With Love, all things and all healings are possible- and in this new era of medicine, complete healing will be possible in body (physical and etheric), mind/emotion, and spirit.

(Tracy Latz, M.D. is a speaker, co-author of *Shift: 12 Keys to Shift Your Life* and *Shift: A Woman's Guide to Transformation*, practicing board-certified integrative psychiatrist, metaphysician, immunobiologist, holistic healer and one of "The Shift Doctors" that can be found at www.shiftyourlife.com.)

"The foregoing generations beheld God and nature face to face; we, through their eyes. Why should not we also enjoy an original relation to the universe? Why should not we have a poetry and philosophy of insight and not of tradition, and a religion by revelation to us, and not the history of theirs? ... The sun shines today also. There is more wool and flax in the fields. There are new lands, new men, new thoughts. Let us demand our own works and laws and worship." — Ralph Waldo Emerson, Nature

Is There a Future for Health Care?

by C. Norman Shealy, M.D. Ph.D.

For reasons that escape me, medical insurance is called "Health Care," despite the fact that from the beginning it has "insured" only partial payment for a portion of medical or surgical treatment and virtually nothing for health promotion or maintenance! Actually, prior to the late 1920s, there was no "insurance" to cover medical expenses. Two hospitals in Dallas introduced Blue Cross which offered 20 days of hospitalization per year for an annual fee of $6.00. In the late 1930s Blue Shield was introduced to cover surgical and some general physician expenses while being treated in a hospital. Initially, many physicians fought against this intruder into their lives and in Oregon, physicians who agreed to the Blue Shield plan were kicked out of the local medical societies!

By the early 1940s, unions began pushing hard to have ever-increasing medical benefits, and even Harry Truman tried to get a National Federal Medical Insurance law passed. Failing that, he and Congress passed legislation that doubled the number of medical students and hospitals. In 1963, Johnson began pushing for Medicare. On my personal stationery, I wrote him a letter stating that he would bankrupt the country, because the government could never do anything that is cost-effective. I was investigated by the FBI and they spent a week trying to get me fired from my position on the faculty at Western Reserve. Medical expenses were 4.5% of GNP prior to Medicare. Within 5 years headlines across the country were screaming "Crisis in health care costs!" which had risen to 12% of GNP. Today, of course, medical expenses are 17% of GNP and WE ARE NOT AS HEALTHY A NATION AS WE WERE IN 1964!!!

By the early 1980s, Medicare introduced one of the greatest oxymorons of all time: Group-Related Diseases. Essentially an ingrown toenail was grouped with an amputation of the foot! The general medical insurance mafia quickly followed suit and increasingly began delaying and denying coverage for many treatments. By the early 1990s hospitals (which had also always had much greater success in collecting from the insurance companies) began buying physician practices and starting their own insurance companies.

Now, finally, Obama-care has become law, with more regulations and hogwash language than the entire internet. It promises nothing except total government regulation of everything from conception to death.

The problem with the entire system is that it has never been about HEALTH CARE!! The most successful national program for improving health has been a 60-year attempt to decrease tobacco use. The percentage of adults smoking has been cut by about 50%. Health enhancing, but not a great record! Meanwhile, Americans have become fatter and less active, so that obesity is now the number one health hazard and cause of premature death. Actually, Dr. John Knowles wrote the most important health article of the century in the late 1970s, "The Responsibility of the Individual." Knowles stated that "99% of people are born healthy and become unhealthy because of human misbehavior."

And indeed, human misbehavior is responsible, conservatively, for 85% of all illness!! Smoking, crummy nutrition, inactivity and excess use of alcohol and drugs are responsible for a huge majority of diseases and probably shorten average life expectancy by about 22 years. The fast food restaurants have contributed greatly to this, as have all food companies that continue to use artificial fats, monosodium glutamate and other poisonous junk additives.

Yes, conventional medicine can produce miraculous "cures" in many acute illnesses and can help maintain some chronically ill people. But, cure and prevention of illness begins with the individual. Sadly, only 3% of Americans have the 4 most basic health habits:
- No Smoking (about 78% of Americans)
- Body Mass Index of 18 to 24 (only one third of Americans)
- Eating a minimum of 5 servings daily of fruits or vegetables (average is 2.3!!)
- Exercise a minimum of 30 minutes 5 days a week (about 10%)

The SOLUTION:
We must make healthy habits a national and individual priority, making personal responsibility the number one goal.

In the long run, we must have ONE major Non-Profit, Non-Government company responsible exclusively for health and medical care. The trustees should be from the public and should have a maximum term of two years. Three allopathic physicians and three allopathic nurses should be coupled with three holistic physicians and three holistic nurses to set the standards for covered Health and Medical Care.

There should be set, standard costs for each participant, with no exclusions, and no "groups" who get reduced rates

Those unable to pay for this should be supported by general taxes paid by all, BUT extra emphasis should be given to these individuals, who should be penalized through their welfare checks until they clean up their health habits.

(C. Norman Shealy, M.D., Ph.D. was the founding President of the American Holistic Medical Association and founder of the first comprehensive pain and stress clinic.

www.normshealy.com)

"...their misfortune is at least in part caused by humanity's collective insanity. It… originates in our attitudes and manifests on the streets." — Brie Liberty

Homelessness, a Sign of Our Collective Insanity?

by Brie Liberty

I'm not personally one of those mentally ill statistics (yet), but I have sure been surrounded by it my whole life. My mother was schizophrenic. My father had Tourette's Syndrome. My sister suffered from depression her whole life. My stepdaughter has a borderline personality disorder. My nephew is bi-polar and had to quit high school. My sister-in-law is schizophrenic, as well as depressed. I adopted my stepdaughter's little girl, who has been diagnosed with Asperger's, and it goes on from there! The good news is there's a happy ending for almost all of these stories.

However, I'm writing this to discuss a related issue. I recently discovered that Walter, a very dear friend of mine, is homeless. I've known this person for over 35 years. It was all so shocking! How could this good and otherwise normal person be homeless?

There was something very wrong about that. Homeless people are the ones you avoid at all costs — the ones standing there at a stoplight holding up signs with their dirty hands, asking for donations to support their pathetic lives. They make me want to cross my fingers, hoping the timing of the light will let me escape getting stuck where they can easily stare right into my window with those pleading eyes.

I've even worried about my safety around them on occasion. However, now I have a fairly realistic concern about *their* safety! How about the fear they must face every day finding themselves homeless with no one to turn to except a few occasional handouts?

Until recently, I thought that most homeless people are just too mentally ill to help. You would think if anyone should understand mental illness, it would be someone with a family like mine! However, I'm just now waking up to the collective insanity many (most?) of us share with regards to the homeless people around us.

I decided to call my friend's ex-wife, who I hadn't talked to in 25 years. She told me, yes, indeed he is homeless. She had found him a while back, but lost contact with him again, so I decided to go on my own journey to find him.

When I arrived at the place where the homeless hung out (a popular place in Santa Monica, CA), I found myself searching all the faces of the homeless, wondering about their stories. I also wondered what his face would look like. I had certainly aged, myself. I could only imagine what *he* might look like!

I started to observe the many homeless, walking around aimlessly, although most were just sitting quietly by themselves, staring at the ground, or sleeping. I began to find myself observing my own prejudices.

For centuries, it has been considered acceptable for society to hide the mentally ill. We all want to run away from them, so they don't clutter our already cluttered world or create more chaos in our already chaotic world. Society has condoned our right to feel this way. While that might be changing, it can't change fast enough for those who find themselves trapped in this vicious cycle of misfortune; mental illness is often a part of that, but not as much as you might think.

I suppose, in some cases, we need to keep a safe distance. However, their misfortune is, at least in part, caused by humanity's collective insanity. It is for each of us to decide how we have contributed to this and — more importantly — how we can help dispel this problem, which originates in our attitudes and manifests on the streets?

As I approached the many homeless people, I knew I had come there needing *them*. I needed their help to find out how this whole homeless thing worked, if I was to have any success in finding my friend. I also needed their help if I was ever to dispel my illusions about them, so I moved around talking to them, one by one.

To my surprise, I didn't find anyone with any obvious mental illness. I'm not suggesting there is none. I'm sure there must be, just as there must be some alcoholics and drug addicts among the homeless. Still, the men I talked to were lucid and engaging. That was an eye opener for me! I also found them to be warm and respectful.

One man sitting on a bench said to me, as I left, "Have a nice day!"

He wanted *me* to have a nice day?? What about him???

They were all willing to help me find my friend, but were helpless to do so, because most of them really don't know each another. They live in the same area, but seemed so isolated from one another. Possibly this is from losing the concept of being part of a community.

Perhaps those living in closer quarters under bridges may have a better sense of community. The one thing I did find that everyone had in common was a profound sense of loneliness and isolation.

There may be much to discover in the hearts of these men and women who try to find communion within themselves. There's probably an even bigger story among those who don't try because they can't. However, I only spent enough time among them to discover there was a deep sense of brokenness, a deep sense of guilt they felt about failing society, and a sense of guilt I felt for society failing them.

I would like to end this story with a happy ending, but I cannot. I'd like to tell you that I found my friend. I did not. I don't know how to solve the tragedy of loneliness and despair, or the economic ruin that tosses good people onto the streets. However, I'd like to suggest that until we find some of these solutions, something will always be very wrong with our world!

The only thing I can offer is that we each work to change our beliefs about those who walk the path of the down and out, as well as those who face mental illness every day in their lives. Perhaps you can tweak your point of view about who they are, or who they aren't. After all, one of them is my dear friend, Walter.

(Brie Liberty took care of her own mentally-ill mother for 12 years. She is a writer, author of the children's book, *The Secret of the Lake*, and has produced children's songs with Roscoe Orman from *Sesame Street*.)

"Clearly, mental health services are needed and necessary. As the world continues to change and accelerate with exponential rapidity, the needs for mental health support will continue to increase dramatically. With the shifting consciousness attendant with planetary changes, mental health can no longer be singularly focused; it needs to evolve and expand to serve a higher vibratory consciousness." — Adele Ryan McDowell, Ph.D.

Mental Health Needs a Booster Shot

by Adele Ryan McDowell, Ph.D.

The majority of mental health practices are deeply rooted in the medical model, knee-deep in the latest edition of the DSM to provide diagnostic labels and entrenched with pharmaceutical solutions. And much of this is aided and abetted by the insurance companies who look to quantify and contain mental health treatment within boxed minimums.

Current mental health paradigms are buttoned-down and frequently running in place to deal with overwhelming demands. They are also near-sighted and narrowly defined — far too constrictive to deal with a world in widespread flux. If mental health is to serve the greater good, it needs to make substantive, systemic changes as well as expand its scope and perspective with a heightened, more inclusive and collaborative consciousness.

Clearly, mental health services are needed and necessary. As the world continues to change and accelerate with exponential rapidity, the needs for mental health support will continue to increase dramatically. With the shifting consciousness attendant with planetary changes, mental health can no longer be singularly focused; it needs to evolve and expand to serve a higher vibratory consciousness.

How can mental health best serve a changing world?

Crazy is not always crazy. Mental health is called to take a broader perspective, where it incorporates an understanding of the noetic, numinous life of the individual. Spiritual crises and paranormal experiences are not the stuff of diagnoses, but an alternative way of being in and of the world.

Mental health practitioners ask, "Do you see things? Do you hear things?" These questions are generally asked to determine if the client (or patient, depending on your theoretical bent) is psychotic. But if I, a trained and licensed professional, were to respond to those same questions, my responses would be yes, on both counts. Am I crazy? I think not. However, I *am* spiritual, intuitive and consciously cultivate my relationship with the invisible realms.

Mental health needs to color outside the lines and value transpersonal experiences and intuition development; demonstrate greater latitude and acceptance for the idiosyncratic expression of the soul; and honor the mystery inherent in the human experience. Dreams, symbols and past-life memories would be viewed as sign-posts, not just collateral residue of a busy day or an overactive imagination. And, of course, imagination — that deep pool of possibilities which pulls from the psyche — would be encouraged and celebrated as a primary response to, and resource for, a changing world.

It is time for the mental health community to increase its collaborative and inclusionary efforts. Good mental health is good mental health, however we get there. Let's call everyone to the table who works in the healing arts and begin a conversation — no more "me against them," allopathic versus alternative. There are many paths to wholeness and wellness; there is much wisdom and expertise to be shared. It is time to collaborate.

Interdisciplinary research has already indicated that exercise and meditation are both effective means in dealing with depression. Acupuncture assists addiction recovery and alleviates pain. Pain can also be managed with hypnotherapy, medication, electrical stimulation units, meditation, guided imagery and the like. Journaling, mindfulness training and support groups have been proven to aid and abet, as well as maintain, weight loss. In other words, there is a panoply of multimodal options that are available. Wouldn't it be wonderful to provide our clients with a number of healing options? We all are aware that not all things work for all people. With an *inclusive* approach, there is hope — and subsequently, healing — to be had with mental health wellness possibilities.

Quantum physics teaches us that everything is energy. Isn't it time for mental health to invite energy medicine to the table? Energy medicine has a successful, centuries-long history, beginning with the work of shamans and other indigenous medicine people. Every culture around the world has its native healers who use their respective talents and gifts — soul retrievals, qi gong, herbs, ritual, community, dance, song, vision quests, fire ceremonies, ritual baths, etc. — to heal the individual or the community. These methods have worked with minimal, if any, side effects.

Accept the dark side. Mental health is quick to medicate in order to take away the emotional pain and feelings. Certainly, medication has its place in the clinical tool kit. However, it is often overused and leap-frogs the client out of the depths of their being into a place of minimal affect.

For example, research institutions are working on developing a medication so that the soldiers who go to war will have no PTSD symptoms. Their memories will be sanitized. How unnerving is that?

Pain and darkness are scary, but like certain bulbs that need weeks of darkness before they bloom, so, too, do we humans need to feel the dark side of our emotional selves so that we can learn, evolve, grow and expand our consciousness.

Asclepius had it right: Creativity is the key to healing. In ancient Greece, within his healing temples, Asclepius and his daughter Hygeia provided a safe place for the weary and wounded to come and find healing sanctuary. There were sleep chambers, incubated dreams, community and expressive arts such as drama, comedy, music and dance. In today's therapeutic environment, the expressive arts such as art therapy and dance therapy are the misunderstood step-children. Perhaps, it's time to take a page from Asclepius and work on healing in soulful manner.

If operating soulfully, mental health would encourage creativity; it is the antithesis of destruction and animates the life force. Plus, the mental health benefits are many. Creative practices develop self-expression, quell anxiety, alleviate some forms of depression, soothe trauma, offer hope, encourage mastery and enhance solution-oriented thinking. And, further, if we view the subconscious material as the key to therapeutic insight, does it not make sense that the less-defended right brain might access subconscious material more easily than its left-brained, linear, sequential self?

The new mental health would emphasize wholeness (the root of the word "healing") and move away from the stigma of illness to the encouragement and enhancement of the soul. It would encourage a whole self for a whole world, where there is innovative thinking, collaboration and a world view where everyone is seen as the magnificent soul they are.

Mental health: Roll up your sleeve; it's time for your booster shot. The world needs you alive, thriving and supporting the shifting populace.

(Adele Ryan McDowell, Ph.D., is a transpersonal psychologist, higher consciousness teacher, and the author of *Balancing Act: Reflections, Meditations and Coping Strategies for Today's Fast-Paced Whirl* and *Help, It's Dark in Here* (2011).

You can find more at www.theheraldedpenguin.com and www.channeledgrace.com.)

"Science is coming to understand what mystics have known throughout history. Future psychiatrists, psychologists and psychotherapists must be trained and initiated into such an understanding to create and utilize a psychotherapeutic model that goes beyond the range of human experience and behavior and which encompasses our connection with our divine nature and the transcendent aspects of our being." — Tracy Latz, M.D., M.S., Mh.D. and Marion Ross, Ph.D., Mh.D.

The Future of Psychiatric and Psychological Training: Approaches to Treatment of Mental and Emotional Distress in the New Era

by Tracy Latz, M.D., M.S., Mh.D. and Marion Ross, Ph.D., Mh.D.

Many psychotherapists have watched patients struggling with their symptoms for months to years and felt the frustration of being unable to change the outcomes through traditional psychotherapy. Historically, psychiatrists, psychologists, therapists and counselors have been taught to evaluate patients in the following manner. First, the patient is interviewed to obtain a thorough history of presenting symptoms of distress (anxiety, depression, psychosis, trauma, etc.), medical history, past psychiatric history, family history, and early childhood/social history to include evaluation for abuse, family of origin dynamics, substance abuse, education, work history, and current relationship dynamics. It is of note that very few psychotherapists take a spiritual history.

Then, a mental status exam is performed to evaluate for attention, concentration, speech, psychomotor activity, memory, mood, affect, thought processes, logic, insight, judgment, thoughts of self-harm or harm to others, and auditory or visual hallucinations. Then the mental health professional decides upon a treatment plan that would most often be a form of either cognitive-behavioral therapy (an intellectualized approach of dissecting the thoughts behind behavior patterns, challenging the distressing thoughts, and creating new non-distressing thoughts to substitute for the old ones to create new behavior patterns) or insight-oriented psychotherapy (an intellectual delving into the emotional story behind the presenting issue) and possibly medication (if warranted) to remove the acute distress.

In this traditional evaluation and approach there is much emphasis on the patient being a victim of both circumstances (childhood and current) and genetics; treatment is focused on treating presenting symptoms without addressing the core issue(s) underlying the stress, depression or anxiety.

With the advent of some of the "newer" psychotherapeutic approaches utilized in the fields of mind-body medicine, energy psychology and energy medicine — such as mindfulness, guided imagery, EMDR (eye movement desensitization and reprocessing) and EFT (emotional freedom technique) — psychotherapists have begun to approach an awareness that a non-ordinary or supra-mental state of consciousness underlies much "illness" and holds the key to experiencing a sense of wellness. Such is the holistic approach of the transpersonal psychologist and the metaphysician who draws upon the sciences of cognition, consciousness, philosophy (Egyptian/Hermetic, Indian and Chinese), energy medicine, social and cultural theory, and the world's spiritual and wisdom traditions.

When utilizing the Hermetic approaches of the transpersonal psychologist, the patient is no longer viewed by the therapist as a victim, but rather as a powerful co-creator in their own life and circumstance. Even more critically, the patient becomes aware of how powerfully they create in their own lives. What each of us do to self-sabotage or get in our own way (with anger, resentment, guilt, shame, self-definition, lack of self-love, heartbreak, sense of inadequacy/powerlessness, feeling unlovable, sense of abandonment, fear of the unknown, and lack of self-discipline) has a bigger impact on our inner peace and experience of joy than any obstacle anyone else might attempt to put in our path.

In order to help non-metaphysically trained people understand how we create in BOTH positive and negative ways in our life, body and relationships, we teach "the Bow and Arrow Theory of creation" in our books, classes and seminars. The Bow and Arrow Theory as to how we manifest is as follows: The bow represents our emotional intention (e.g. anger, resentment, fear, love, compassion). The strength of the emotional intention determines how powerfully we draw back our bow to send our thoughts out into the world to manifest. For instance, if there is not much power behind the emotion, then the arrow will scarcely fly. If, on the other hand, there is great power behind the emotion (such as rage), then the arrow will fly quickly and can create rapidly and profoundly in our lives.

The arrow represents our thought, which directs the intention. The thought will direct how the intention (or great emotion) will actually manifest in our life. It is important to note that we cannot create for anyone else. We can only draw back our own bow to create in our own life. If we draw our bow back with the intention of harming others, we will only draw similar negative energy into our own life. If you have conflicting intentions (such as "I want to lose 10 pounds," but then, seeing a plate of chocolate brownies, think "I REALLY want one of those brownies!"), the most powerful intention will win out to create in your life.

The holistic, transpersonal psychotherapist sees the whole patient: mind, body and spirit. Thus far we have addressed only the mind and body aspect and tend to leave the spirit piece to the pastoral counselors. An understanding of esoteric or energetic anatomy assists in understanding how flawed any approach is that leaves out any one of the triad of mind (thought/emotion), body (physical) and spirit. We are multidimensional, transcendent, spiritual beings, expressing through physical matter. However, the energetic layering of expression is as follows: (A) the higher vibration of the spiritual energy of our soul must express through (B) the filter of the lower vibration of thought and emotion that we hold around us (created by ego and our perceptions of our experiences), to then energize or give life to (C) our physical body — to create a sense of either wellness or disease. Therefore, an approach that acknowledges and encourages a connectedness to something bigger than us is helpful, whether that be to God, Source, Spirit, Universe or Nature.

Science is coming to understand what mystics have known through-out history. Future psychiatrists, psychologists and psychotherapists must be trained and initiated into such an understanding to create and utilize a psychotherapeutic model that goes beyond the range of human experience and behavior and which encompasses our connection with our divine nature and the transcendent aspects of our being. We need to train therapists to assist the patient to "get out of their head" and "into their heart," to access their own intuition and transform the faulty thought patterns that can cause emotional trauma, depression and illness. The ancient mystery schools trained their initiates to understand this and to implement such healing for others. It is time once again to teach these philosophies, tools and techniques to our psychotherapists, who can in turn teach it to their patients that are willing to take such an approach and accept some personal responsibility for their own health and well-being.

"I observed the prayers of every religion rising to the heavens from the Earth. Each religion's prayer represented a color of the rainbow and they all ascended to the heavens. It was a thing of profound beauty, and the lesson I took from this experience was that all people's prayers which emerge from a sincere place in the heart are accepted by God, regardless of their religion." — Perry

The Future of Religion

by Perry

My old friend, Hunt Henion, asked me to write something about the future of religion for his new book. Although I am not considered an authority on religion in this day and age, Hunt was aware that I was identified in playing a significant role in founding the religion of Islam as a guide to the prophet Mohammed, as well as being identified as playing a significant role in founding the branch of Judaism known as Hasidism and, in a later lifetime, helping to found the State of Israel. So I guess one could say that religion is in my soul and it is from that place I will speak on its future.

Let's first start with a story.

When I was around 24, I started practicing lucid dreaming. This practice led to a vivid dream, which I later understood to be an out of body experience. During this experience, I was taken by two angels to visit the higher realms and shown many things that are written about by mystics in various texts.

I observed the prayers of every religion rising to the heavens from the Earth. Each religion's prayer represented a color of the rainbow and they all ascended to the heavens. It was a thing of profound beauty, and the lesson I took from this experience was that all people's prayers which emerge from a sincere place in the heart are accepted by God, regardless of their religion.

My own personal thoughts about religion are that everyone has a religion; by my definition, religion is a system of beliefs that people adopt and practices that they adhere to which best express those beliefs. Therefore, any "ism" (including atheism) is a religion. Whatever someone's chosen religion is, it is my view that they have a complete right to their beliefs — that God gave us free will, and no human has the right to interfere with it.

I believe that each person should be free to develop their own particular belief system, and then test how their belief system works in their life and in the greater world as a force for good.

My own observation of life informs me that if I conduct myself according to the following principle, it seems to attract more harmony into my life. The fundamental principle that I strive to live by is the "Golden Rule":

"Do unto others as you would have them do unto you," or its corollary, "That which is unpleasant to you, do not do to others."

This belief was certainly delivered to humanity via the religions, and when it is applied with diligence, it seems to result in a more balanced, happy and peaceful life for its practitioners.

Perhaps, underlying the "Golden Rule" is what is known as the "Law of Cause and Effect" or the "Law of Karma." This law instructs that whatever we project into the world in thought, action and expectation, is ultimately reflected back to us in our life experience. In other words, "We reap what we sow."

In order to mitigate against the Universe reflecting back to us the negative that we project out into the world, the "Golden Rule" was given. It essentially protects us from the darker aspects of ourselves.

Another benefit of the "Golden Rule" is that it acts as an instruction manual on how to receive positive reflections from the Universe which will come our way as a result of our decision to consistently project positive thoughts, actions and expectations into the world.

The Law of Cause and Effect encompasses creation. The Universe was *created* — it is an effect that arose from a Divine Cause. Human creativity operates in the same manner and is subject to the same principles that created the Universe. We humans have the potential to create a better world if we intentionally decide to employ our creative capacities in this direction. It is apparent to me that there is currently a lot of promotion of the use of human creativity for the benefit of the individual's wants, which to me seem primarily ego-driven.

The bigger "Secret" yet to be revealed is the untold benefits to humanity that could be accrued if we were to use our creative capacity to serve our soul's/higher self's will, especially if we work collectively. This is the "Secret" of how to create Heaven on Earth.

Besides the Golden Rule, religion has also housed the tool of ritual for humanity. Many rituals were adopted from the cultural practices that existed prior to establishment of organized religions. Much meaning can be derived from performing rituals that mark the key transition points in people's lives, as well as the changes in nature's cycles.

We live in "interesting times": technology has advanced more rapidly than the wisdom required to guide its use for the benefit of humanity. This sorry situation has had the effect of deepening the longstanding religious and economic divisions that now plague our planet. The effect on the environment and on human health has been particularly significant.

On a more positive front, scientific advancement is beginning to bridge what were once separate fields. Science and religion are now being bridged by advances in the field of consciousness. The nature of the soul and the existence of God, which were once the domain of the mystics, may one day just be accepted scientific truths unworthy of debate.

Coping with the ever-accelerating pace of change can be very challenging for many people. This is where ritual can be very beneficial. Rituals can provide grounding and positive benefits to mind, body and spirit if they are practiced in a disciplined fashion.

Rituals connect us to our heritage, ancestry and, very importantly, to Mother Earth and God. Another benefit of rituals is that they can be performed in groups, and this brings people together, which is healthy in a world where people tend to physically isolate themselves more often than they did prior to the creation of the Internet and other modern conveniences.

The philosopher, Martin Buber, stated: "God exists in the space where people are present for each other in relationship." To me, this statement represents the highest potentials embodied in religion today and in the future. When people of shared belief come together in relationship and are present for each other, then God's presence on Earth is made manifest.

I suggest to today's religious leaders that when people of different religious beliefs come together in relationship and are present for each other in shared prayer and ritual — the full expression of God's unity and diversity is made manifest, and the glory of Heaven is literally brought down to Earth. This is the beautiful gift that religion can give to the world in the future.

My call to the religions of the world is to fully recognize and celebrate their unity under one God, to remember that what makes a rainbow beautiful is the range of colors that exist in absolute harmony within it. The same harmony can exist on Earth as it does in Heaven, if every color on the rainbow peacefully remains in its place.

(Perry can be found at www.healingjourney.biz.)

"The cooperation and compromises we need to 'change Washington' will not happen until 'we the people' demonstrate that it can be done in our local communities. Wherever we live, we must model it before we demand it of others." — Paul Von Ward

Reclaiming Government by the People

by Paul Von Ward (11/20/10)

For the past fifteen years I have focused my work on interdisciplinary, historical/scientific/spiritual articles and books. However, our increasingly complex society makes it clear that we cannot discuss the human potential and our place in the cosmos without considering the values and methods that shape our communal institutions. The requires our attention to the politics of government.

Based on my early career as a military officer and government official, I wrote my first book, *Dismantling the Pyramid: Government by the People*, 30 years ago. Although it is now out of print, it is perhaps more relevant today than when I wrote it.

In calling attention to that book, I reveal the personal part of the story — not because I'm proud of it, but because I believe all of us gain insights along the way that can be useful later in life. My story began more than 50 years ago, when I became a part of our government and political system.

As young Congressional interns in Washington, Bob Graham (later Governor and U.S. Senator) and I represented a new Florida "political protege" program. In 1959, we met President Eisenhower and Senator John Kennedy, among others.

We interns learned how our Congressmen responded to their constituents' needs, at least enough to insure their re-election. We also witnessed the early stages of a growing, pernicious cadre of corporate and special-interest-group lobbyists arriving in Washington (and had sumptuous dinners with some of them).

Today, that cadre of corporate lobbyists is literally the 4th branch of the American government. This "institution" is crucial to the success or failure of a bipartisan deficit reduction strategy to keep the United States from going bankrupt.

This became apparent when leaders of the President's commission confronting the challenge released their draft ideas in mid-November 2010. The resulting furor stimulated all parts of society, particularly corporate and special interests who benefit from the status quo. This motivated me to write about my view that the problem cannot be solved by those who created it.

Back to the story: Returning to Florida State University, I continued my youthful interest in student and local politics, but then felt drawn to some sort of national service. The following year I voted for the John Kennedy who had inspired me as I attended his Senate committee hearings.

As so many thousands of others like me, I was inspired by his challenge to "do for the nation." With Vietnam a dim image on the horizon, I aborted my doctoral plans in psychology, took a Master's degree, and enrolled in the U.S. Navy's officer candidate school. After three-and-a-half years of active duty, with a pending assignment to command a "Swift Boat" on the Mekong, President Johnson appointed me, along with a couple of dozen 20-somethings, as new Foreign Service Officers.

As the intern from rural Northwest Florida, I was a very naive idealist, but much of what I learned in the subsequent thirty years can be found in *Dismantling the Pyramid*. (A PDF version of the book can be purchased at http://www.vonward.com/websitebookorders.html.)

It was written in 1980, the year I resigned from my FSO position in the U.S. Department of State, frustrated in my efforts to do the job I had both chosen and had been assigned to do. Our federal institutions were clearly out of step with our nation's self-declared destiny. During my private non-profit work for 15 years in Washington D.C., I saw further decline in governmental integrity and its increase in self-protection and self-perpetuation continue for another fifteen years, and things have only gotten worse since then.

In both my government and my private (but "governmented") work, I was dismayed by experiences in what we called the "iron triangles," which benefit all of the players: government employees, Congressmen/women and their staffs, and the corporate/non-profit private sector. Working in synch, we established mutually reinforcing flows of power and funding, regardless of their benefit or irrelevance to society's most pressing needs. This doesn't mean all is wasted, but large chunks of it only benefit a few.

I served the State Department in four overseas assignments. However, the part of my work that is relevant to this story occurred while I was in Washington. A few senior officials in the State Department and the Civil Service Commission wanted to stimulate a movement to reform the way "inside Washington" worked. They believed a few public servants, coupled with research on human psychology and organizational theory and strong political leadership, could make "Washington" leaner and more effective. They hoped that, with outside professional advice, rising young officers in key departments could be catalysts for reform.

As part of that initiative, I was sent to Harvard University's MPA program to study research on government renewal and to work with scholars who might serve in advisory roles as our reform initiatives got under way. Suffice it to say, our reform strategies did not succeed.

At this point, I must make it clear that many individual government employees are dedicated public servants who also recognize the problems described here. Most elected and appointed officials start with high ideals, but the system conditions people to compromise in many situations in order to keep their perks.

While I think change can "start" from inside, I still believe, as I did in 1980, that the needed reform of our overblown, deadlocked, national government cannot succeed unless the President and the Congress are shown a new direction by a "deeply-rooted consensus" of fired-up citizens from all levels of society.

In *Dismantling the Pyramid*, I proposed a nationwide movement similar to the Committees of Correspondence idea developed by Massachusetts Samuel Adams prior to the American Revolution. This group's cooperation among the 13 colonies helped to create the confederation that led to our independence as a nation.

A citizens' effort like the recent Tea Party activists' early initiatives had such a potential. However, that movement came under the control of the corporate and financial interests who could benefit from its voters providing cover for their agenda.

Conversely, it is the "civil society" that must insure government officials and financial elites in all sectors are held responsible for the overall public interest. This kind of a civic-minded government, with the public's best interest at heart, had been the objective of our Civil Service System created (along with subsequent legislation) in 1872 to replace the "spoils system."

In the old system, government employees supported the politicians who arranged for their jobs. The Civil Service goal was that all except a few appointed officials would fulfill their responsibilities based on professional merit and would remain apolitical. Our evolving human nature, manifested inside and outside government, has made that goal unattainable.

Since the 1900s, we have only added new layers of bureaucracy onto increasing fragmentation of government functions. As new programs are added, old ones are left to their own devices, with regular tax-payer transfusions to keep them alive. No one applies public tests of continuing relevance or effectiveness. Officials are afraid to prioritize to make sure pressing new programs replace out-dated offices and staffs. They simply ask Congress for more money for it all. Keeping these outmoded or low-priority functions going continues because each has its special interest groups lobbying alongside federal staff on Capitol Hill.

After World War II, several initiatives were taken to reduce its size and revitalize the federal bureaucracy by eliminating unnecessary jobs and wasteful programs. The 1947-48 Hoover Commission made an unsuccessful effort. Subsequently, Lyndon Johnson and Richard Nixon initiated abortive government reforms. Jimmy Carter was the last President who attempted (tepidly and failed) to address the kinds of fundamental problems that produce bureaucratic bloat and overly expensive programs. Since then, Presidents have had little influence over an overweening bureaucracy, a deep-pockets lobby, and partisanship that immobilizes the Congress. This special-interest system produces national laws and administrative regulations that directly benefit their financial backers.

My view on this problem goes back to a cost-saving project I was given as a young officer in the U.S. Navy and similar research in my Washington jobs during the 1970s. It was reinforced by 15 years of work in the government-supported private sector. I came to the conclusion that about 30% of the personnel and administrative resources of every department was simply wasted. This wasteful redundancy does not include the recent findings of inspectors-general reports on egregious waste in defense and other agency contracts in wars, overseas programs, and domestic programs. Keep in mind that what auditors call waste is really money in the pockets of corporations and contractors who in turn donate part of it to Congressional campaigns.

The results are departments and agencies focused on self-preservation, overlapping responsibilities, and strong fiefdoms that are literally unmanageable. Nobody is really in charge. To avoid rocking the boat, everyone takes the easy way out. This overly expensive government, particularly given its tawdry benefits to the general public, pays for a behind-the-moat bureaucracy, largely directed by officials acting as surrogates of the financial backers who insured their election or appointment.

Thus, we have created a self-perpetuating institution that we call Washington Government. Its implicit purpose is to maintain its octopus-like arms as mechanisms to convert and re-allocate large percentages of the nation's common resources (its human labor, nature's riches, and citizens' creativity) to a small percentage of U.S. citizens and international corporations. This process does not only involve the transfer of general tax revenue. Even more important is the use (or non-use) of regulatory power to economically favor certain groups, particularly the largely amoral financial and corporate sectors.

These modern-day elites are much like the self-centered, parasitic lords and ladies who surrounded the kings and queens of old Europe. They will betray others and their own integrity to keep their "royal" and financial status. To avoid something like the French Revolution, a few goodies are given to the working and poor parts of the electorate through bogus tax breaks and social services. This makes them feel they get something for their passive support for the status quo and deters them from investigating the huge subsidies given to the most wealthy few.

In this lapse of values like equality and fairness, no one can now stay behind personally comfortable walls with people like ourselves and ask someone else — politicians and other "leaders" — to solve the problems that we all let fester, thinking we were immune to catastrophes that only affected others. The cooperation and compromises we need to "change Washington" will not happen until "we the people" demonstrate that it can be done in our local communities. Wherever we live, we must model it before we demand it of others.

Only private citizens can develop a new consensus about the future role of America in the world and its collective responsibility for the use of our common heritage to benefit all Americans and the world at large. All of us must learn again that when a singular government becomes the central orchestrator of a complex society and distorts its laws to benefit the few, it will kill "the goose that lays the golden eggs."

Best wishes for your initiatives in your own community. When they flourish locally, they will connect with similar ideas, creating the consensus for a New America.

Paul Von Ward

Email: paul@vonward.com
Websites: www.vonward.com and www.reincarnationexperiment.org

"Can spiritual practices strengthen our ability to connect, either personally or in business, and create a bridge to take us beyond 2012? Yes!" — Camille Leon

Blending Spiritual Values with Building Businesses

by Camille Leon

Just days before this, I had set an intention in my meditation to meet more like-minded friends. There are no coincidences. In Tracy Roe's introduction to her Examiner.com interview with Hunt Henion, Ph.D., a spiritual author, she talks about her initial meeting with him. This story shows us the linkage and importance of blending our spiritual practices with our business decisions in a vivid way. However, it also points to the difficulty of finding professionals who share our values and creating a community that supports us in our work.

Can spiritual practices strengthen our ability to connect, either personally or in business, and create a bridge to take us beyond 2012? Yes!

It took a family health crisis to help me see today's disconnection between holistic professionals and those who are successful in business. When my grandmother and mother had separate issues, my research led me to hidden alternatives — hard to find because those who are grounded in spirituality often avoid the process of buying and selling. They are uncomfortable with "business as usual."

Frequently, they fall to one extreme or another: too shy to share their value with a world that doesn't understand or too passionate in their delivery to accept that some are not ready yet.

In order to address these challenges, we must ask ourselves key questions that will bring us together and enable us to communicate with those around us. Then, we can unite with each other and assist those who need us most.

The Breakdown of Business

When did we get so disconnected?

Wasn't there a time, not so long ago, when business luminaries and politicians also had families and philanthropic activities that kept them grounded? After all, Andrew Carnegie is known for his success in business and in philanthropy. Carnegie is known for setting Napoleon Hill on a journey that would impact the success of millions. The Kennedys are still recognized for their charitable endeavors. Yes, they had their dark sides; however, nowadays, many corporate powerhouses seem even more out of touch with themselves, their families and the rest of the world. The old economic structures are crumbling before our eyes and bringing much of the world down with them.

Let me suggest that this downward spiral started accelerating on 9/11/2001 when business, government, families and individuals all came to a screeching halt. Instead of going to work that day, we were watching an event that should have been the trailer for a new Denzel Washington movie, rather than in the news and in our living rooms. Sadly, since then, rather than turn the tide, we've seen leadership at major companies (including Enron, Tyco Toys, MCI Telecom and Goldman Sachs) make decisions that created scandals with far-reaching side effects in both the energy and financial markets. More recently, oil giant British Petroleum (BP) made choices that led to an environmental disaster whose long-term consequences far outweigh any potential gain that could've been hoped for. The fallout from these events has reverberated globally as well as into our personal economies.

Toward a Replacement Structure

"Out of the ashes of crisis, corruption and public distrust, a grassroots movement to revitalize the ethics and Spirit of free enterprise is gaining momentum and attracting millions," says Patricia Aburdene in *Megatrends 2010*. Slowly, the seeds of a new economy are taking root.

When renovating a building, it is fairly simple to demolish the old structure before building the new one. Unfortunately, when considering solutions for a world of people on a planet that is ecologically stressed, the process is more complex. New organizations and structures need to be planted first so that individuals and businesses have options available immediately.

At its most rudimentary level, business is simply the exchange of money for a service or product. It is another form of bartering: If you were a master carpenter in need of a pig for your family's meal and your neighbor already had a house (having no need for your services), what could you exchange for the pig? Thus it became necessary to create a medium of exchange.

These days, of course, the almighty dollar has become something that many value for its own sake, rather than for its value in terms of quality of living, health and happiness. In other words, we've become disconnected from the original purpose of money — as an equal exchange.

In the late 1600s, Quakers became successful in business because of their ability to blend their values with practical applications that worked (and still work) in the world of commerce. In Peter Jackson's *BBC News* article of 1/20/2010, we are reminded that some of the oldest and most successful companies are firmly rooted in a community that merges personal ethics with "real life." Ironically, it is because of their non-conformist views that they were forced into starting businesses. As non-Anglicans, the Quakers were barred from universities as well as many civic and public offices. Although it is not generally known, companies including Barclays and Lloyds banks, Clarks shoes, and chocolatiers Cadbury (now owned by Kraft) and Rowntree are just a few of those founded by members of the pacifist group.

What is holistic?

As we move into 2012, the need to balance short-term results with long-term consequences is becoming even more important.

How do we find like-minded professionals and practitioners who can help us find the "soul-lutions" that will sustain us?

Can we reach out to the people who need us most and speak to them in terms they understand and embrace?

Finally, is it better to come from a position of love or of judgment? When I am brainstorming with colleagues and discussing the merits of values-based business, I have to remind myself that each person is in a different position on the continuum. In defining holistic and sustainable alternatives, it is helpful to leave room for others to join me, no matter where they are starting.

We can begin by connecting with like-minded friends and colleagues who help us come full circle.

"Holistic" is not just about health and healing, or even mind-body-spirit. The best holistic professionals and businesses, whether they are attorneys or bookkeepers or healers or coaches, consider long-term consequences as well as short-term results. While physical, emotional and mental health are critical, most of us are better off when our legal house is in order, our environment is clean and our financial accounts are safe as well.

To maintain lasting balance, it is critical to blend our spiritual values with our business practices and lead the world in replacing a worn-out economic model with new, sustainable structures. This is true for solo professionals and practitioners as well as for those who represent holistic values in larger corporations.

(Camille Leon is the Executive Director of The Holistic Chamber of Commerce, a growing community of professionals, practitioners and business people who support each other in blending spiritual values with building businesses and helping consumers find holistic solutions.

For more information or to become a Member, please visit their web site at http://www.theholisticchamberofcommerce.com.)

For the New Era: the New Land Ethic and a New Tax Ethic

by Wendell Fitzgerald

The most pressing problem of economics is why there is so much poverty and struggle to make a living amid so much wealth and progress. We humans now produce more than enough to alleviate all poverty, yet starvation, economic suffering and social upheaval caused by recurring economic collapse persist. The current dysfunctional economic episode starting in 2008 has marginalized tens of millions of people, even in the wealthiest of countries. Something is clearly not working.

Economic systems historically have not delivered on the promise of benefiting all people because the Earth, land and natural resources have become monopolized in the hands of a few individuals, national elites and — in the modern era — corporations. Small holders of land (including most homeowners and small farmers) have owned much land, using it productively and efficiently by any standard, but today statistics show that 85% of the most valuable land and natural resources is concentrated in the hands of only 3-5% of the people. The land held by its monopoly owners is often not used productively or efficiently, thus depriving people who need it and would use it well if they had access to it, driving them into poverty even while driving up the cost of all land. This means all of us have to pay fewer and fewer people and their corporations for access to our own planet; they become wealthier while masses of people are deprived of the opportunity of making a living for themselves in a sustainable manner on good land. This applies to land in all countries, not just underdeveloped ones, and is the root cause of virtually every social and economic problem.

Land ownership *per se* is not open to question, so monopoly of the Earth is never questioned. But the question that must be asked is, "Whose Earth is this?" This is the known as the "land question." The question is not whether land should or should not be owned, but rather to whom should the payment for access to land be paid?

The good news is that the income from ownership of land and natural resources is an unearned income. This is so because owners of land do not create the Earth and they do not create the value of their particular pieces of it. The community of all people creates the market value of all land. This is understood by all economists who bother to explore the issue, as well as by the real estate industry and mortgage bankers who enable the practice of buying and selling the right to collect this unearned income. There are other sources of unearned income in the economy, but the unearned income from land is, always has been, and always will be the largest, by far. The fact that land is sought in order to hoard it and speculate with it — in order collect a value its owners do not create — is unconscionable, since land is an absolute necessity of life for every human being without exception, the deprivation of which means poverty and death.

The actual and imputed income from ownership of land, excluding the value of and income from improvements on land, amounts to 25-30% of income worldwide. This amounts to tens of trillions of dollars every year ($3 trillion in the U.S. alone), and this huge sum is growing with the increase in population and the progress of technology that makes land or what can be done on land more productive and therefore more economically profitable.

The private collection of the community-created value of land has always enriched the few at the expense of the many. The future prospect of being able to do so has always given rise to land speculation. It is the root cause of the monopoly of land over many centuries and the ongoing land and natural resource "grabs" that continue at a furious pace today, and which deprive humanity of its natural social safety net.

The result is the paradox of poverty and economic struggle for the majority amid great material progress and great wealth for the few. The monopoly of capital is enabled by this free lunch handed to the monopoly owners of the Earth. Monopoly of capital would not exist to the extent that it does without land monopoly.

The failure to include the land question in analyses of economic, social and environmental problems is THE cause of the failure of analysis, because the land question is more fundamental than all the other questions. Policy makers, pundits and public intellectuals who never even mention the issue when pontificating about the crises humanity faces do not appear to be in touch with reality. This may seem somewhat harsh and judgmental, but is it not so?

The simple solution is to require all land and natural resource owners to pay to the community a "land rent" valued at its current market price, every year via appropriate forms of taxation for the land that they own, whether or not they USE it productively or efficiently. Please be clear that most homeowners and small- to medium-sized farmers USE their tiny bits of land very productively and very efficiently, and for this reason they would ultimately pay less and fare better than under the current system. The largest percentage of revenue to be collected in this way would come from large land and natural resource owners and because of this, the tax on community-created land values would be quite progressive (taxing those most who can most afford to pay), with the further advantage of not being avoidable.

As taxes on land values rose, all other taxes on earned income from labor and capital could and must be reduced and ultimately eliminated.

This is a necessity in order not to increase the overall tax burden, but also because of the fact that all government services increase the value of land and nothing else but land value. Since government services only make land more valuable it is only reasonable and just that landowners per se be required to pay the full cost of these services. Otherwise they are subsidized at the expense of all other taxpayers.

The existing property tax is one mechanism (among others) that is already in place in many nations to accomplish what is needed. The simple technical solution is to eliminate all existing property taxes on man-made improvements and increase the tax on land values to collect the same amount of revenue. When the property tax is shifted to a land value tax only, the tax rate on land values can be raised to the point where it equals the yearly rental value of land. This will allow all other taxes on labor and real capital used and invested in the real economy to be eliminated.

There may be reason to keep some user fees (such as we now pay for public transportation) and some taxes to achieve environmental or other worthy economic or environmental goals (such as carbon and fuel taxes), but essentially all other taxes and fees for public services that most of us pay could be abolished.

This would be the core of a new land ethic which recognizes and enforces the common ownership of land and natural resources merely by requiring payment by individuals and corporations for the privilege of exclusive USE of OUR land. Property titles to land would not be disturbed in any way and no new regulation of how land was USED would be necessary.

Not only would this generate enough revenue for governments, but it would have the effect of ending land speculation thus ending the boom/bust real estate cycle (which is only about land speculation, since improvements do not go up in value). All urban sprawl caused by land speculation would cease. Cities would backfill and rebuild themselves into more compact and livable environments, constantly renewing themselves as needed, unhindered by the penalty of taxation on new and rehabilitated buildings and earned income from them. The purchase price for land would be driven down by the tax on land values and thus the cost of housing would be reduced and stabilized. Less mortgage money would have to be borrowed from banks. Unemployment and poverty would dissipate with the increase in economic activity. Small businesses would be encouraged, along with the new jobs they create. All of this would be physically confined to more compact cities. These results have occurred where and to the extent that land values have been taxed more heavily in concert with reduction of taxation on improvements. This theoretical construct has thus been proven in practice.

People would have to get used to the fact that they could not depend on the increase in the value of the land under their homes or other real estate investments to enable them to finally retire. In exchange everyone who works and/or invests in the real economy, freed of taxation, will be able to earn enough through productive activity to prosper and save for retirement.

We can have real sustainable economic growth within the human community and not at the expense of the environment. Those who want economic growth and those who want to stop economic growth should take note of this. Economic growth can occur and be environmentally sustainable as long as land and natural resources cannot be speculated with or give rise to unearned income. Such is not possible under existing land tenure and tax regimes, all of which are based on promoting and protecting those who get something for nothing, which *must* be at the expense of people and the environment.

This is the new land ethic many have been hoping for. It is also the new tax ethic. Together they safeguard private USE of land and titles to property in land, but require humanity to forego buying and selling the Earth merely for profit. The Earth will no longer just be a commodity like soybeans or coffee. Buying and selling of land will only be for the purpose of enabling proper and efficient USE of land, and not for profit in itself. In one simple yet profound set of public policy shifts, humanity would share the Earth by sharing the value that all humanity gives to her.

For further information, search the Internet for references to Henry George, the 19th century American political economist and social philosopher, who clearly articulated these ideas and whose modern adherents have brought these ideas up to date. Also research terms such as land value taxation, economic rent, land speculation and other terms used here and look to see where these ideas have been put into practice.

For a good source of all this information, see an online course by going to www.course.earthrings.org. A donation (none of it going to the author) is requested for full enrollment, and it will be money well spent.

(Wendell Fitzgerald has been a student of fundamental economics for more than three decades and is currently the president of the Henry George School of San Francisco.)

"It is vital to raise awareness that youth throughout this world are realizing — and are being called forth to reveal — that there is a global consciousness attempting to arise in the hearts and minds of humanity. This consciousness is what is being called the 'spiritual revolution' or the evolution of humankind into full awareness." —
Dr. Nina Meyerhof

Youth as Spiritual Activists for Social Change

by Dr. Nina Meyerhof, president of Children of the Earth

Spirituality is key to transcending political, dogmatic, and religious boundaries.

It is vital to raise awareness that youth throughout this world are realizing — and are being called forth to reveal — that there is a global consciousness attempting to arise in the hearts and minds of humanity. This consciousness is what is being called the "spiritual revolution," or the evolution of humankind into full awareness. We are learning from science that we are interdependent and interconnected as one life. We are beginning to understand that peace can exist not only as a state of being, but also as the manifestation of a way of creating peace in our world. It is in our unity that we will be able to accept our diversity and finally find the means to live together here on Mother Earth.

Below are the guiding principles that Children of the Earth promotes in order to encourage the personal and world-changing transformation we all want:

- Trust your intuition.
- Demonstrate dignity and respect.
- Communicate with honesty and clarity.
- Assume the good intentions of others.
- Support shared leadership.
- Celebrate diversity.
- Be inspired to take risks.
- Allow decisions to emerge and embrace the process.
- Understand that the whole is greater than the parts.
- Strive for actions based on selflessness and love.
- Support sustainability, both personally and environmentally.
- Honor agreements and take ownership for outcomes.

Hear the call for UNITY as a child of the ONE life.

Our Code of Ethics derived from the indigenous peoples of the world. These ethics are for us to live as just, compassionate, loving human beings.

Ethical standards for human development derive from a great sense of wonder that we are all members of the same human family, connected in the web called spirit and sharing one Earth.

- LOVE — for the form, voice, thoughts and spirit of each person.
- RESPECT — for differences.
- HONESTY — of our feelings, thoughts and behaviors; to be transparent.
- TRUTH — in feelings and thoughts.
- COURAGE — to take a stand.
- HUMILITY — to reflect inner peace.
- WISDOM — to be a seeker.

Programs of Children of the Earth

Our programs consist of Social Action Chapters and Spirit Youth Hubs. Social Action Chapters are youth humanitarian projects conceived as a result of an inner transformation. Spirit Youth Hubs are groups of youth who meet to focus on spiritual explorations and intentions. Our goal is to support and link young people as a global family of humankind for a conscious and flourishing future.

Youth come to us from all corners of the world, recognizing and remembering hope — hope that we can live as a human family on our planet Earth and beyond. Youth tap into their inner life and reunite with their true spiritual nature, and this reflection leads to a sincere ethical life.

In this process of reaching within and experiencing one's nature — beyond self-esteem and basic needs and desires — they find the place within of uniqueness and solid character where personal identity connects to the universals of life. Once recognized, these universals are then bestowed upon one another as a given right with responsibility for a life of purpose and meaning. In the universal consciousness there are no differences of color, race, culture or national intent. The universals are simply that we all want to love and be loved, to be free of need and desire, to be true and empowered, and to live a life of meaning.

Spiritual Activism is a concept that originates from the understanding that youth have incredible energy, which may be channeled into potentially living a life of the Will to Good and for positive social change. This understanding is based on seeking inner peace and a connectivity to the consciousness available to us all, that youth can and will activate their calling for a life of meaning reflected through daily actions and service for the greater good. This the Children of the Earth's model.

1st Step: Inner Quest for the Authentic Self

As one goes more deeply into the self, the understanding grows that one is not defined by one's surroundings of parents, culture and religion. Rather, inside dwells a loving human being, seeking full expression.

2nd Step: Deep Compassion for the Other

Next we become conscious of how we can best express ourselves in the world for the highest good. Transforming conflict, using language that recognizes the other, appreciating without judging can occur when one no longer judges oneself. A sense of union occurs that can be called love or spirituality in action. We begin to act as part of a whole, building "Oneness" rather than asserting the separate ego. A sense of union occurs that can be called love or spirituality in action.

3rd Step: Interconnectedness for Global Unity

The third process is based on the recognition that there is a global community of young people who await connectivity with you. All are the new leaders of this evolving consciousness for social change. They share a growing awareness of how to live as stewards of all life. From this new consciousness, there will be new models of how to live in our world and more importantly, there will be a secure human future.

Conclusion:

We dedicate our work to the building of a better future. Our programs are to support young people with the empowerment and leadership skills necessary to advance peace in the world. Together we build networks of cooperation, multicultural understanding, spiritual values, and ethical living skills.

(Dr. Nina Meyerhof, president and founder of Children of the Earth, has made a life of advocating for children and youth. She has received many awards for her work, including The Mother Theresa Award, the Citizens Department of Peace Award, and The International Educators Award for Peace to the Vermont State Resolution as Peacemaker. Nina continues to focus daily on altering world views for creating a better future.

http://www.coeworld.org)

Visions of the Future

"The passage through 2012 is guaranteed to be exhilarating and rewarding for those whose attitudes and state of mind are resonant with living up to their full potential and being of service."
— Cynthia Sue Larson

When Consciousness Changes the Physical World

by Cynthia Sue Larson

I feel extraordinarily fortunate to be living through this time of converging realities that invites us to literally walk between worlds. The realities each of us experience can be quite different than another's, as each person's frame of mind selects the reality they encounter. The passage through 2012 is guaranteed to be exhilarating and rewarding for those whose attitudes and state of mind are resonant with living up to full potential and being of service.

One of our biggest opportunities post-2012 is to realize all of reality is a dream, and we are the dreamers; this special state of consciousness of being awake while dreaming is known as lucid dreaming. I once had a lucid dream in which I reclined on a grassy green field on a sunny day, gazing up at the sky. I noticed the sky seemed different, because instead of seeing a full moon in the sky, I was looking at a full planet Earth. I thought to myself, "If I'm looking at a planet Earth in the sky, what am I on right now?" Clearly I was on planet Earth, so how could I be seeing another Earth? I then watched in awe and wonder as I saw hundreds of planet Earths converging in the clear blue sky above. This was a slow transition, about the same speed as a solar eclipse, as these planets moved closer together. "What is going on?" I wondered aloud in the dream… realizing as soon as I asked this question that I knew the answer. This is a time of convergence, when it is as easy to walk between worlds of intention and attention, from one reality to another, as it is to cross a creek by stepping from stone to stone.

We select the worlds we walk through in accordance with our state of consciousness — our emotional attitude and intellectual mindfulness — bridging the gap from one space-time to the next. People encounter positive conscious reality shifts when in alignment with matching intentions, from their heads down to their toes. A sense of clarity comes from holding such a state of alignment, as one becomes more honest, compassionate, and aware of observing the roles we play in human dramas. Anyone sustaining such energetic alignment while simultaneously energized and relaxed can experience life as a waking lucid dream, in which everything they think appears around them in the physical world. In sharp contrast to such a life of instant manifestation, many people operate more like a funky radio frequency, broadcasting three or more conflicting signals in a noisy jumble.

Shifting reality by walking between worlds can be exhilarating. Since my spiritual epiphany and kundalini experience in 1994, I've seen all kinds of things appear, disappear, transport and transform. I've watched burns, cuts, and blisters vanish instantaneously. I've pulled dollar bill after dollar bill from in my wallet until I'd taken a handful of dollar bills from a wallet that a few moments earlier had no dollar bills at all. I've seen car keys, a small crystal, and a tooth my daughter lost at school appear out of thin air. I've witnessed spontaneous remissions of cancer, instantaneous healings of broken bones, and a dead cat very much alive again. I've seen people and cars appear and disappear out of and into thin air, books change their content, a gigantic sun dial sculpture appear where it had not been before, and restaurants with completely new interior decor that have supposedly "always been that way." I've heard a carton of milk land heavily inside my refrigerator. I've watched rain start and stop as I thought "Start" and "Stop." I've seen lights turn on without anyone touching the switch. I've found lost items in places that had been empty moments before, and have been seen by others to be at places I've been daydreaming about.

Tremendous advances in awareness have been achieved over the past decade, as reality shifts became increasingly commonplace. In a RealityShifters survey conducted in April 2000 with 395 individuals, 95% stated they experience synchronicity and coincidence in their daily lives. A majority of respondents felt that noticing reality shifts has changed their attitudes (59%) and beliefs (55%), and 45% felt that noticing reality shifts has changed both their attitudes *and* beliefs. 86% of the respondents reported, "I've experienced time seem to slow down, stop, or speed up." This experience of noticing changes in time is essential for encountering a state of "nowhen" outside the regular flow of time, which we sometimes feel when daydreaming. This "nowhen" is felt in a Oneness state of mind, as the "eternal now" point of view adopted by shamans and spiritual masters, allowing consciousness to shift gears from one particular space-time reality to another.

In the remote viewing exercises I've led to view what lies beyond 2012, most participants clearly sensed feelings of tremendous harmony, peacefulness and joy. Some also sensed that just past this peaceful calm lay some degree of chaos, stress and strife for others. For the most part, the energetic view of 2012 feels like a smooth continuation of life as we know it today, with an awareness of higher energies that facilitate instant manifestation. Most remote viewers saw themselves in peaceful solitary contemplation on December 21, 2012, sometimes looking out across a large, calm body of water. I saw myself by the Pacific Ocean along the California coast, sensing that even as I basked in radiant vibrations of unconditional love, many people on Earth were focused primarily on material matters, such as windstorms.

Humans will encounter overlapping realities and worlds post-2012, as we experience shifts in reality in accordance with our thoughts and feelings. This period of global transition is a time when multitudes of parallel realities converge in such a way that some people will experience a reality of peace and plenty, while others experience chaos and lack. With so many worlds to choose from, people have a unique opportunity to learn how our state of mind and consciousness plays a vitally important role in creating our reality.

We will live in worlds that are uniquely keyed to whatever personal levels of love vs. fear, internal alignment vs. internal discord, and external harmony vs. external disagreement that we embody at any given moment. This time of converging realities provides unique opportunities for medical researchers to discover that the most important factor in healing involves our underlying beliefs, spirituality, attitude and mindfulness.

Physicists will recognize and report the primacy of consciousness in all aspects of reality, and acknowledge that the effects of consciousness necessitate a restructuring of the scientific method and a review of past experimental results. In the midst of global economic, meteorological, and social instant karma, an underlying sense of higher values will emerge as people feel a sense of global unity and compassion. I envision a world of caring people who increasingly respect all aspects of creation, genuinely wishing for what is best for one another.

People will see themselves clearly with appreciation and awareness of all roles being played out, and an underlying knowledge that none of us is defined solely by gender, race, religion or social class. People will increasingly feel a sense of divine unconditional love, and relate to one another heart-to-heart with the awareness that we are all as one, and that dreams are real. We will more easily think, speak and act harmoniously in alignment with the spirit of oneness that unites us all and inspires each one of us uniquely."

Life post-2012 requires each of us to maintain clear and open heads and hearts, in order that the reality we get is the one we want to have. Our ability to ask for and receive inspiration to rise above personal limitations can assist us in facing and managing our shadow issues — those qualities all humans possess, which need to be cleared at this time of instant karma. It's good to have a spiritual practice, with high ideals that you do your best to live true to at all times, in order to intend and maintain a state of internal cleanliness. The level of integrity I recommend is akin to knowing and being OK with the idea that everyone can read your mind, in a state of emotional and spiritual integrity sometimes referred to as transparency.

The biggest invitation to life post-2012 is that we can have a greater sense of awe and respect for the underlying essence of reality. This sense of awe is inextricably intertwined with a feeling of deep love and appreciation for all of creation. We can feel every physical experience and interaction in life is a great gift. While many crises will require our attention and assistance, we can see that everything on Earth is moving forward beautifully. It is up to us to remain open to inspiration, and open to love. As singer/songwriter Michael Stipe from the musical group REM sings, "It's the end of the world as we know it, and I feel fine."

(Cynthia Sue Larson, MBA and intuitive life coach, is editor of the monthly RealityShifters.com e-zine and author of several books, including the highly acclaimed *Reality Shifts: When Consciousness Changes the Physical World*.)

December 21, 2012: The Great Adventure Begins!

By Rev. Rhonda Smith, Ph.D., D.D.

December 21, 2012 is a day of transition. It does not mean that you will awaken on December 22, 2012 and everything will have changed. On the other hand, in a sense, it *will* have changed. The group consciousness will have changed its perspective from "I" to "We." The beauty of "we" is that the "I" remains as it blends with All That Is.

The work actually begins at this time, although much work has already been done to help move everyone onward. So how will this new world of "we" manifest? No one really knows. However, I can make some suggestions to focus on in order to manifest them. Those in the new positions will be there because of proven abilities, not birth or connections.

Let's start at the top. We'll call this the "royals". They consist of presidents, monarchies, etc. Many of those in this position see the people as servants. That is backwards because their position is to serve the people. To reverse this, those who fill this level will be highly evolved, enlightened people who have fully opened to receiving information from the "rest" of themselves — the higher planes. They will function from a place of complete purity and humility. Their role will be to see the correct direction for humankind, to guide, to inspire and to enlighten.

The Communication level would be next and have two parts. Those would be the arts and the media, which are currently used to produce propaganda to maintain the upside-down system that exists now. The artists will be those who possess the ability to see into other dimensions and realities, to pull in inspiration and ideas, and then manifest them in works of art on the physical plane. They would create art with the intention of educating and celebrating the evolution of humankind. The media side of this would be those who have developed the ability to communicate and possess a love of expressing the TRUTH. They would provide the dissemination of enlightened information, giving humankind ALL the factual information to allow for fully informed choices, which encourage evolution.

Let's look at Resource Management. Right now the resources are mostly being used and distributed for the benefit of the few "at the top." Those involved with this will be working from their heart and feel a kinship with the Earth, so that they work WITH nature to create abundance. They would help ensure an abundant supply and preserve all natural resources. They would also handle the distribution of the basic raw materials needed by industry. One of their first projects will be to find and distribute the already existing sources of free energy.

Now to the Banking level. At the moment the banks have control of commerce and do not concern themselves with the welfare of the people. They currently do such things as funding development in less developed countries where the people and the land are being abused. This level will be composed of people who easily align with willpower (self-control) and can structure a fair method of barter and exchange because they have a gut feeling for the operation of society and they listen to it. They will create a currency and system based on gold or some other higher-vibratory substance, rather than one based on debt, which is what currently exists.

Then there is the Industry Level, which is currently interested in profit over people. This level will consist of those who can invent, design and engineer technology to improve society. Obviously, this level would include what we now separate as industry, technology and science. Their job would be to provide the basic necessities (goods and services) needed for the well-being of humankind, so people can focus as much attention as possible on their growth and evolution to their fullest potential.

Let's talk about the Military level. Right now they are used as soldiers to continue "power over," rather than warriors who know that fighting and killing is the LAST resort, not the first. First of all, this level would be used defensively and ONLY as a last resort. It would consist of those who are well-grounded in the natural order of society and "feel" when things are out of balance. They would have the discipline and power to help restore that balance. This is not about "right" or "wrong," nor is it about imposing another's choice on someone. It is about cooperation in the exercise of this power.

Close to this is the Government level. Currently it's composed of misused power and manipulation. It will work behind the scenes as a coordinator, much like a conference organizer, for all the other levels. If it is working properly, quietly behind the scenes, everyone will be aware of the brilliantly run society it supports.

Finally, we look at the Religious level, which currently endorses a polarized set of moral rules to encourage guilt, separation and fear, overarches everything and wants to have "control over" everything. If you study the religions, you discover that this was not their initial intent. This level will also work silently behind the scenes. Although the Bible says man shall have dominion over the Earth, it was never meant to be a license for misuse, which unfortunately has been the case. This will change to the perspective of oneness with everything, reverence for the Earth and all the life she fosters. Humankind will recognize that everything is infused with Spirit.

From these changes in perspective we create the enlightened society for all of humankind — the society where every resource is used for the greatest good to all, so that every basic need of the individual is provided. This moves us all out of "survival" and takes us to "living." When we are out of the survival mode, we are able to concentrate on developing our potential. When we develop the individual's potential, we all benefit and evolve and become the true human beings we are.

"You'll know the shift is commencing for you when everything begins to look more luminous. (Those who are not in harmony with the Earth will never experience this.) Colors will appear more vibrant. Things will seem to glow and have auras. As the planes overlap, you'll begin to see things from the higher dimension." — Hunt Henion

Our Shifting Awareness

by Hunt Henion

Awareness of our shifting reality rises as the Earth's resonance frequency rises. Our vibrations also rise as we're pulled up by the Earth's rising vibrations, and as we respond to the same influences as the Earth, such as gamma rays. Vibrations are rising faster all the time, but so far, it's been a fairly steady rise.

We were told in channeling that sometime after 2013, Planet X will fly by, the magnetic poles of the Earth will flip, and then the actual Earth will probably shift on its axis some. This will cause a rush of energy in the Earth and its vibration will increase greatly in a short period, just like we might experience a rush of adrenalin during an accident.

Our vibration matches the Earth's increase, throwing us into "reset mode" as we approach "phase conjugation" (the point at which the wave vibrations come together to manifest a new physical and spiritual reality). When the magnetism drops precipitously and the poles shift, we may experience 20-30 hours in a re-set mode as all thought stops except for an awareness of our unity with all things. It's said that this takes place in what we'll experience as a black void. After this, we'll all have a much higher vibration. Yet, that's still not the widely anticipated ascension.

There's confusion because the "phase conjugation" that sends us to a new dimension (either lower or higher) has always come during this period in the void when this has occurred before. However, this time people have a choice, and it needs to be a peaceful experience. So, after all the physical excitement, there'll be a period to regroup. This is where people either let their consciousness soar with the new natural order Mother Earth has chosen, or discipline themselves to stick to what they know is right, thereby confirming their life contracts in the 3D world.

During this time, the Earth's vibration should stabilize around 13 on the Schumann Resonance scale, and everyone's personal vibration should be resonating at about that same level. We were told in channeling that we'll probably all have our original 12-strand DNA restored on our subtler levels by then, too. (It probably won't be physically restored, but be well on its way to that.)

Sometime, shortly after that, the shift goes into full motion and things start to really get interesting. Personally, I feel the shift will finally culminate about a year to a year and a half after Planet X flies by.

You'll know the shift is commencing for you when everything begins to look more luminous. (Those who are not in harmony with the Earth will never experience this.) Colors will appear more vibrant. Things will seem to glow and have auras. As the planes overlap, you'll begin to see things from the higher dimension.

You may see fairies and animals that you don't recognize. You may notice that you can communicate with them. Hopefully, you'll notice that they're friendly. Eventually in the newly evolved world, just like the world in which nymphs and fairies live, there won't be carnivores anymore. However, for the time being, you can take comfort in knowing that the consciousness of the carnivorous animals that evolve with the Earth will be evolving just like us. So, especially with our enhanced communication with them, there really shouldn't be any reason for fear.

High protein plants will also quickly evolve, and all carnivores will be converting to vegetarianism before too long. This will take place because of the complementary nature of the two suns, the new one being what we call Comet Holmes today. This energy from the two suns will also affect our biorhythms, allowing us to live longer and healthier lives.

The closer we get to the actual shift, the more unusual things will happen. As our vibrations rise into a harmonic that is not compatible with people who insist on their three-dimensional reality, those people will appear to suddenly vanish right before your eyes. From their point of view, we'll also suddenly become invisible.

Just before the shift, people may start looking different too. This is partly in the eye of the beholder, but it's also partly because those evolving with the Earth will begin to manifest their light bodies over their more familiar forms. After the ascension, almost everyone evolving with the Earth will eventually be getting a complete makeover. We'll be healthier and appear younger in most cases.

As dramatic as all this seems, because it takes place over several years, the general population will probably never know what's happening — demonstrating again that reality really is an individual creation. Make yours a magnificent one!

(Excerpted from the best-selling book, *Looking, Seeing & Knowing* by Hunt Henion, www.shiftawareness.com)

A Visit to the New Earth

by Sylvia Bucek

On July 11, 2010, suddenly and out of the blue, I was transported to an unspeakably beautiful dimension that I could not describe in words except to think I had somehow been beamed into Heaven. Gradually, it dawned on me that this must be a New Earth, and that I was an immortal child coming into being. I wondered if I had died. No sooner did the thought come to mind, than I saw/recalled how that world began to fade away.

I came back thinking that I had experienced a drill, like a "test flight," as we head towards the year 2012. I had foreseen this event three decades ago during a near death experience that had opened my mind to the inner kingdom permeating all life. I realized then that my death was nothing more than the withdrawal of consciousness from the lower mind's perception of reality, whereas my Higher Self was showing me a worldview based on eternal life that one is always free to return to. Though "return" is perhaps a misnomer if one were to embrace the idea of being a thought seed from the Mind of God — a soul growing up in the world and blossoming into the consciousness of Heaven on Earth in the beautiful Garden of Eden.

In a small way, I have known this all my life and have attempted to express it through art and written works. One of the characters I created is a human flower child named Rose who loves all Creation and recognizes her unity with all living things. In relating to a flower, she recalls the tiny seed's struggle through the underground, and she knows how it feels to ascend to a new dimension above ground, always reaching toward the heavens to become all she can be. These days I can see how this analogy might also apply to our collective ascent into a new world. Now that the third-density human drama is being played out, I am taking my cues from Nature and learning to navigate within the natural world, though in essence I have been here all along.

My earliest memories recall my deep love of Nature and appreciation for all things natural, including those that would otherwise be termed supernatural. As a child I grew up in a true-to-life wonderland and thought everyone else did, too. I thought we all lived in a magical world among angelic beings that come in all shapes and forms and that we all loved one another. I believed it was common knowledge that animals communicate with us and that we commune with flowers and trees and otherworldly realms. Back then, I was unmindful of the veil between the heavenly strata and physical plane, nor did I know about the rift between man and the natural kingdom. Had I wondered about it, I might simply have thought that there is so much more to life than meets the mortal eye.

At age ten, in my mind's eye, I saw that as a human being I was predisposed towards a consensus reality that appeared to be dead-ended, but my Higher Self was showing me that the human is essentially an immortal being on a spectacular journey to Heaven on Earth. Yet it seemed to me that part of the journey looked like an altered reality where it was possible to lose sight of one's natural self and become lost in a virtual world. (In my ten-year-old mind's eye, I was seeing a vision of my future near death experience that showed me dying).

To the child in me, it looked as though my adult self had disconnected from a dream-like illusory world and restored the Soul connection to this moment, which was somehow taking place outside linear time. My Higher Self was showing me that in order to stay in touch with one's natural self, one simply needs to Be, (referring to one's Soul Being), and that in time, anything else falls away. I anchored the moment in my mind, like an icon that encapsulated the entire vision. The icon simply shows a little girl in a yellow bathing suit, standing in crystal clear water beneath a cerulean sky. Next to her head is a thought balloon, like you'd see in a comic strip, showing her adult self returning to that moment as though she were coming down from a mind journey that appears to be fading like a dream.

Fast forward to July 11, 2010, and my "test flight" to Heaven — or a new kind of Earth that may have had its basis in the childhood scene described above, in that I was aware of being a child who was entering a state of consciousness that is one with its greater self, whereas the world as I had known it was fading away. Gradually it dawned on me that I was a human Soul coming into Being.

At first, I was too overawed to talk about my experience, nor would I have known where or how to begin. The only scene I could compare it with was Jody Foster's trip to a heavenly dimension in the movie, *Contact*. Although I had no idea how to explain my "flight," it nevertheless felt as though I must, but how does one express the ineffable?

Intuitively, I packed a few things, including pen and paper, and — along with my cat Heather — retreated to a wilderness cabin in a woodland setting on beautiful Round Lake, Ontario. I had felt hesitant about bringing my pet along. The woods around the cabin are home to many chipmunks and my cat is a beast of prey, but leaving her in town with a sitter was not an option when I went to close my suitcase and found Heather snuggled inside it. So the first thing I did, upon arrival at the cabin, was to ask the angels to please guide the chipmunks away from Heather. The result was astonishing. My elderly and otherwise rather lethargic cat seemed to wake up to the memory of an idyllic reality where everyone lives in happy co-existence and folks do not eat their fellows. It was very sweet, seeing the chipmunks going about their daily business as my huge orange cat played in their midst.

Naturally I found myself tuning in to my own childhood and the innocence I had known. Although my favorite food back then had been meat, I was too little to understand the disparity between my love of animals and what I ate. As far as I could tell, we all lived in a magical world of sweet love and sunshine forever. But I was born in 1941 and a world war was being fought. So of course it was not long before I heard life on Earth crying for help, and I prayed for a way that I might help.

My Higher Self answered by showing me a vision of a kind and gentle world, peopled by angelic beings who love all Creation and are here to help anchor Heaven on Earth. To the child in me, the vision was simply a sweet love story told by my angel about the enchanted life that we all live in. On the other hand, to my adult self, it seemed that in many ways I was growing up in a brutal world in which my job was learning to become utterly harmless.

I learned that, inherent in our nature, is the ability to transcend the lower self and ascend to a higher state of consciousness, just like dying and waking up to the angel within. I learned that the human DNA is encoded with our journey to the glorious new dimension that is dawning, and that it can be downloaded (God willing) when we are ready to receive it, according to the Divine Blueprint that is now being unveiled.

In my book, *Flight Manual*, the key-sized guide is a caterpillar whose DNA is encoded with the journey to its new dimension of life on Earth. Like us, all the caterpillar needs to do is stay connected to the conscious, cosmic life force that pervades all things from the smallest micro level to the macrocosmic whole. In the end, it emerges from the chrysalis in its butterfly form, taking flight in the new world and touches down in Paradise.

(Sylvia is an artist, writer, animal rights advocate and vegan chef. She is the author of *Flight Manual: 2012, A New Beginning*
www.flightmanual.net)

"Humanity is poised to ascend to the next level of consciousness and awareness. All it will take to get there is a little nudge in the right direction. That nudge, however, must come from us. No one can do it for us and no one can give us a magical key. Each of us must look within our own heart and see what it is we want. We must decide for ourselves, because only when we have decided will we be able to fully embrace our decision and the change that is to come." — E. Dee Conrad

The Road to Tomorrow

by E. Dee Conrad

What will the future look like and what does it hold for humanity? With all the hype around 2012, this is a question many are pondering today, most without any definite answers because it is really up to us. Whether our future holds a magical awakening or a step back to the Stone Age is up to us and the decisions we make NOW about how we as a group want to proceed.

Nothing is written in stone, so any vision of the future is mere speculation at this point. However, speculation is certainly not a waste of time, since focusing on a possible outcome can help make it a reality.

One possibility is that we live up to our full potential and take our place as co-creators of the universe. We — humanity — recognize and come to terms with our full potential as beings of enormous creative ability. Humans helped create the universe and everything in it. The universe did not "just happen" — it was not a random event. There was a plan and we were, and still are, instrumental in executing this plan.

A second possibility is that we will experience a bit of a setback as far as evolution of consciousness is concerned. A "setback" is not so much a regression, as a temporary pause in forward progress. There are those who are hoping for massive destruction for their own gain, but their numbers are small and their power is weak. Then, there are others who are living in absolute fear and dread of 2012, but there is no need to be afraid or worry about what will happen in 2012 and beyond. All will be as it should be — as we want it to be.

Humanity is poised to ascend to the next level of consciousness and awareness. All it will take to get there is a little nudge in the right direction. That nudge, however, must come from us. No one can do it for us and no one can give us a magical key. Each of us must look within our own heart and see what it is we want. We must decide for ourselves, because only when we have decided will we be able to fully embrace our decision and the change that is to come.

Over the next few years, the world economy and its political structures will be flipped upside down. There is a great revolution coming, but it is not the kind where people march in the streets (although that will occur). No, the revolution that is coming involves our perception of reality and who we really are. You might call it a "silent" revolution because the battle for discovery — enlightenment — will be waged inside, not outside, each of us. It will change society forever, but it will not bring discord or trauma. Instead, it will bring unity the likes of which humanity has never experienced. It will bring an end to bloodshed and violence. It will bring humanity back to its essence — its true self — and along with it a new age of existence for the universe as a whole.

This change will bring us to a new level of existence, a level that has never before been seen on this planet. This change will alter our perception of time, space, matter and reality in an instant. One day we will be standing here wondering what all the fuss is about and the next we will have transcended into a world beyond our current comprehension. We will find ourselves in a world where existence is not measured in temporary accomplishments or trophies, but in lasting and permanent grace with full understanding of evolution, existence, and the laws of nature and the universe. For the first time, we will see our role in the universe. We will understand why we are here, at this moment, and why everything has happened as it has. We will see the connection between our life and that of our neighbor. We will see the instant link between our thoughts and our reality. We will understand why our thoughts matter and how our emotions shape the world around us. We will see with perfect clarity who we are and all that we can be — all that we were meant to be. We will experience our true magnificence.

(E. Dee Conrad is the author of the best-selling book, *New Dawn Awaits*)

The Transformation of the World

By Sheldan Nidle

As the dark approaches its defeat, we must discuss with you what is to happen. Once in power, the new regimes will take into custody the members of the previous dark governments. This will free up the "airwaves," allowing a true and open dissemination of information concerning all aspects of the incoming new reality: general debt forgiveness; distribution of tax refunds; delivery of prosperity funds; new monetary system; creation of global peace and nuclear disarmament. After these are thoroughly explained to you, the subject of us, the Galactic Federation, must be discussed. Indeed, the end of the UFO cover-up is a major issue all by itself. We will be introduced alongside the revelation of a whole slew of secret technology. As you can see, a great deal of information is to be released to you in a relatively short period. Also, most of those who were incarcerated for non-violent crimes are to be released after a review of their cases. Lawyers will be retrained and the entire court system overhauled.

The new institutions will be people-oriented. At present, governments, banks, places of work etc., are all geared toward serving the wealthy and powerful, as they have been for centuries. The daunting task of our Earth allies is to turn this attitude on its head and transform the dismissive indifference of your social institutions. We have talked long and hard with our Earth allies on this one subject alone. Special transitional organizations are needed in order to move from authoritarian and hierarchical institutions to decentralized and people-friendly ones. Some of your more forward-thinking corporations have adopted this approach, and this is a good start. However, we favor a complete reorganization of governance along these lines. The average citizen must be able to provide input and, where appropriate, be able to monitor and oversee the changes agreed to. This can be a start for employing fluid group dynamics.

Interaction between government, institutions, and citizens needs to move onto a decentralized footing. Interpersonal communication is set in general to change immensely. Not only does your environment rely heavily on electronics and the Internet, but once abundance sets in, this too will change the way you relate to each other. Further, you are in the midst of a huge shift in consciousness. To top it all, we are about to be added to the mix, and this will create something unique. This coming environment is utterly different from your present one. Moreover, it will be based on one simple fact: personal sovereignty with full unalienable rights. These various rights cannot be abridged! What we are asking our Earth allies to do is simply to make your organizations user-friendly and environmentally responsible. In a nutshell, the new regimes are to change how governments, banks, and corporations respond to you.

     The goal is to create a prosperous, informed, and concerned citizenry. This diversity can solve any problem that comes up. You are to receive great wealth, astonishing technology, and a super-abundance of information. Plus, you are approaching the point of becoming fully conscious! We are here to monitor this and to mentor you when needed; however, the bulk of the responsibility stays with you. Each of you possesses innate wisdom and Heaven's blessings. Your future is bright and the sky is literally the limit! You have enormous resources and a living planet to protect. Included in this is the vast realm of Inner Earth. The Agarthans are part of your world, and like you, they have a huge reservoir of wisdom. Come together to make a wondrous new reality!

     What lies ahead of you are the first challenges of your new star-nation! We know that you are destined to succeed in all that you do. You are a great people! 900,000 years ago, Heaven sent the best and brightest of fifty human star-nations to Gaia. Your ancestors were then co-opted by the Atlantean elites and fell into limited consciousness. For 13 millennia you suffered, learned, and survived. Now the time comes for you to take up the mental cudgels of your frustration and transform them into a glorious and merciful Love that will be the cornerstone of your transformation into full consciousness. Alongside the Agarthans, we await the moment to make ourselves known to you. The magic instant will be when you let go of your past and take on the mantle of who you really are!

     Today you stand on the precipice of a new reality! This new world will be a fully-conscious one, filled with an ongoing series of wonders you can barely at present conceive of. There is an entire solar system to be readied for your guardianship and your exhilarating destiny! Know, dear Ones, in your Heart of Hearts that the countless Supply and never-ending Prosperity of Heaven are indeed Yours! So Be It! Selamat Gajun! Selamat Ja! (Sirian for Be One! and Be in Joy!)

(Excerpted from Update by Sheldan Nidle for the Spiritual Hierarchy and the Galactic Federation, September 28, 2010)

Sheldan Nidle has been a contactee since he was toddler. He is the founder of the Planetary Activation Organization, whose philosophy is to empower the individual in order to transform the world. http://www.paoweb.com

"In the past many of us have kept our spiritual lives separate from our work lives. Now we need to 'be' ourselves in all areas of our lives, bring our spirituality to work and live our values and truths."
— *Colin Whitby*

A Conversation with My Future Self

by Colin Whitby

One way of finding out how we did and what we created for our future would be to go there and have a look round, a kind of fanciful idea until you realize that all this work we have been doing to create our crystal being, our new bodies that naturally radiate the frequency of love, has led us toward a state of oneness, and a state of timelessness.

So travelling back and forth through time is not quite as farfetched as some folk have suggested. In fact, we have only categorized it as fiction because we don't think it happens. So, what if I invite my future self to come have a chat with me about how we created our new world, and what kind of place that is, and maybe take me on a tour of one or two parts of this amazing creation?

I sit down and meditate to move into the appropriate vibration, as one thing I have noticed is that my future self vibrates at a much higher frequency than my present self. This in itself is quite encouraging, as my future self feels very similar to some of the higher-vibrational beings that we have been meeting on our journeys, such as the Arcturians, Sirians, Lyrans or Hathors.

Future Colin (FC) is now approaching, but before we can talk I am being held in a much higher vibrational field by a group of angels. They are the Seraphim, and I was introduced to them by Rev Karen Leys (Ashanti). FC is suggesting that we are much closer to our Angelic selves in the future, and that I should step into their vibration, as I am one of them.

I love this idea. It's something I read for the first time on Karen Bishop's web site, she says that we are Earth Angels and are learning, or remembering, how we return to our natural state of being here on Earth, which is our Angelic frequency. I breathe in these frequencies, greet the Seraphim and thank them for their loving presence.

It is now possible for me to merge with FC and as we do, I feel totally connected with the loving bliss radiating from him/us as he takes me forward into the future. I am being advised that this feeling is our natural state, and we no longer need to keep moving from our 3D vibration to this higher one. In fact, we can stay in our new crystalline bodies all the time. When I look at my body, I'm very light. I constantly radiate a loving frequency and feel totally connected to All That Is. This feeling is reassuring, as many still find this connection only fleetingly. Yet, here we are in the future happily connected to All That Is in a very ordinary way.

Where we live

I'm being taken to a garden, which seems to be attached to a dwelling. The feeling here is one of complete unity with the garden. All the flowers, plants and trees know me, and we greet each other through the heart. Again, there is such a feeling of harmony. I can feel their essences and their connection with Gaia, our Earth, and I can feel her happiness as I walk through this beautiful natural environment. I stop to have a conversation with some of nature's Devas that look after the garden with me. We exchange such a loving heart connection that I feel joy and appreciation radiating from everything, including myself.

As I move towards the dwelling that seems to be my home, I'm struck by how well it sits in this environment. With no jarring shapes or materials, it seems to almost grow out of the ground. However, it is thoroughly modern in appearance. So much light radiates from it, but no signs of our traditional lighting. I suspect we have found a way of creating structures of organic technologies that are completely at one with their surroundings. These structures feel sentient as they have a presence, a consciousness. (We are learning now, that all things have consciousness, even the computer I'm using.)

This conscious dwelling greets and welcomes me, as we both connect through the heart. Our connection gives me joy and appreciation.

Relationships

As I step inside, I meet a group of people who are having a kind of welcome party. They knew my future self has gone to meet me, his past self, and that I'd be coming back with him. They embrace me as I enter. Our hearts immediately connect, and we share amazing love. Whilst my present self finds this quite exceptional and completely blissful, they assure me that this is quite normal here in the future. We always relate to one another through the heart and with unconditional love. I am reassured, for I have always wished that the world could be a place where we could all connect openly and with our natural frequency of love.

The group suggests we go for a spin in our organic ship, another co-created sentient technology, which moves us from one place to another. I say move rather than travel, because as we step into this wonderful "being," our ship, we all connect to "her" through our hearts, think of the destination, and then we arrive. I only feel a kind of shift to the left and back to the right, as if we had moved out of one location and into another. We step out and, sure enough, we have moved to the center of a very modern city, I feel that sense of unity again. All the buildings and technology around me are organic and sentient, and part of the overall loving intelligence of the Earth and all who live here.

They tell me that the city is part of a grid of crystal cities all around the Earth, where we meet and co-create. There seem to be temples and other large crystal shaped buildings, as well as many smaller buildings to explore in future trips.

Oddly there is a lack of clarity regarding what the buildings are for, how we trade and how we interact with each other on a daily basis. I ask why that is, and they say that part is up to us now. We are the creators with many potential realities that we can create whatever we like.

So what happens now?

I'm definitely coming back for another visit, but next time I'm going to bring some friends and co-create the details. Better still, why not start now? Why not start creating our new reality today? There is no time like the present. In fact, there is no time … oh, I forgot to ask how that works!

— Colin Whitby

(In the past, many of us have kept our spiritual lives separate from our work lives. Now we need to "be" ourselves in all areas of our lives, bring our spirituality to work and live our values and truths. Last year had massive energy shifts that moved us into a higher vibration. Colin, an energy route-finder and mapmaker in this new light, assists people to navigate this wonderful ocean of awareness.

Colin@themagicofbeing.com
http://www.Themagicofbeing.com)

"Slowly, as you awaken more and more, you are increasingly attuning your consciousness to the frequency of the fifth dimension by releasing fear and choosing love. Within this consciousness, you are naturally loving and united with all life. Hence, you expect to fill your day with beauty, creativity, en-JOY-ment, gratitude and unconditional love. " — The Arcturians, channeled by Suzanne Lie, Ph.D.

Being Fifth-Dimensional

by Suzanne Lie, Ph.D.

We are the Arcturians, returning to assure you that you are fully grounded in your fifth-dimensional reality. Yes, you are NOW fifth-dimensional. We feel your confusion because life seems much as it has in the past. Except, the ever-present fear diminishes more and more each day, and the drudgery of mundane life is awakening to new and exciting potentials.

You may not understand how you can still perceive the third-dimensional conflict in your surrounding world. But, did you not perceive the second-dimensional plants and the first-dimensional stones while your consciousness was only third-dimensional? Your new life is not limited to the fifth dimension. Instead, your consciousness has expanded to embrace it, while you can still perceive and experience the lower dimensions.

Because you are new to fifth-dimensional Earth, you are creating that which is familiar and comforting. Only after you are fully aware of your emerging Divine Creativity, Infinite Knowing and Unconditionally Loving SELF will you venture into that which appears unknown, yet increasingly familiar. Meanwhile, you are likely overcome with fatigue. Strangely enough, this fatigue only occurs when you believe you must attend to your mundane chores.

On the other hand, once you close your eyes to meditate, even for a moment, the fatigue is quickly replaced with a new feeling that you can't quite identify. This feeling is a sense of completion. You are complete with your experience of the third dimension. You are confident that you no longer need fear and limitation to force you into change. You have proven to yourself that change cannot be forced, anymore than you can force a flower to bloom or the Moon to rise.

But, when did you cross the threshold into this New Earth? There was no fanfare or race to the finish line. There was no defining moment in which you arrived. No! Your arrival has been gradual, like the dawning of a new day. Indeed, you are experiencing the dawning of a new life, a new reality. The lines of demarcation from your "old" reality to your "new" one are not firm and unwavering, for you have not left your old life. Instead, you have expanded beyond it.

Your experience of reality oscillates with your state of consciousness.

When your consciousness is expanded, your attention lies primarily on your fifth-dimensional life. On the other hand, when your consciousness becomes constricted to the habits and chores of your third-dimensional life, your perceptions are restricted to the physical world. Yet, even in your most limited consciousness, you are realizing how quickly your thoughts and emotions are manifesting.

It is because of this instant manifestation that you may choose to "lag behind" in the familiarity of your old life until you feel more confident in your ability to live as a Master of Energy. To have every thought and feeling become a reality is a huge responsibility.

Therefore, especially when you are tired, sick or under stress, you may choose to remain in the third dimension where your thoughts are not instantly manifest, as they are in your fifth-dimensional reality. On the other hand, when you are being creative, enjoying loved ones or in a safe, love-filled environment, your consciousness expands again to embrace the fifth dimension. Therefore, you may feel as though you are living in two realities.

Slowly, as you awaken more and more, you are increasingly attuning your consciousness to the frequency of the fifth dimension by releasing fear and choosing love. Within this consciousness, you are naturally loving and united with all life. Hence, you expect to fill your day with beauty, creativity, en-JOY-ment, gratitude and unconditional love.

Because of these expectations, your expanded perceptions are coming online. These expanded perceptions, also known as "psychic abilities," are allowing you to more easily perceive the resonance of fifth-dimensional life. As you experience fifth-dimensional New Earth, the flow of unconditional love, joy and gratitude guide you to choose to listen to your SELF and make choices in your life that disallow the "hard work," limitations and need for personal recognition, which separate you from the flow of fifth-dimensional life.

In fifth-dimensional realities, there is no need for recognition from "others" because there *are* no others. Everyone is ONE. The recognition that is needed is your own recognition of your Multidimensional SELF. Your SELF will guide you through the complex process of expanding your reality to encompass all that you have known, as well as all that you are creating in the NOW.

Eventually, "all that you have known" will so completely integrate into your fifth-dimensional consciousness that your third-dimensional life will be a distant memory. This process is much like looking back on your childhood, which created the foundation for your adulthood. However, you have grown beyond it and no longer "live there."

Once your consciousness is fully grounded and centered on fifth-dimensional Earth, you can assist awakening ones in the lower worlds. This experience may be much like "living in your home," which is fifth-dimensional, then "going to work," which is in the third and fourth dimensions. You can also choose to experience the many fifth-dimensional worlds in which your Multidimensional SELF simultaneously holds form.

Please feel free to call upon us when you find that your concentration on the fifth dimension is wavering. All you need do is send us a call, and we will assist you by "fueling your earth vessel" with unconditional love. In the fifth dimensional-reality that you are simultaneously creating and returning to, fearful thoughts, feelings and actions will no longer be a part of your life. We say "creating and returning to" because the fifth dimension is beyond time and not limited by space.

You can choose to perceive and participate in creating fifth-dimensional Earth to experience the ultimate act of Divine Creativity. On the other hand, you can choose to calibrate your consciousness to the NOW of the ONE in which fifth-dimensional Earth already exists and has always existed. In fact, in one moment you can focus on creating the fifth-dimensional Earth. Then, in another moment, you can focus on the infinite NOW of fifth-dimensional Earth. You do not leave to become fifth-dimensional or return to your third-dimensional self. Your light holds the third and fifth dimensions as ONE, for the distance between Light and Light is ZERO. Hence, once you bond your consciousness to Light, you are at Zero Point between the light of your fifth-dimensional SELF and the Light of your third-dimensional self. Only illusion separates you from your SELF, as third- and fifth-dimensional light is continuous.

With the release of illusion, all that remains is the Truth, which is: YOU are a Fifth-Dimensional Being!

(The Arcturians, through Suzanne Lie, Ph.D.
    www.multidimensions.com
    www.suzanneliephd.com)

"… the outcome of this cycle is assured …" — *from SaLuSa message, August 20, 2010*

Helping You Meet Your Goals

by SaLuSa, channeled by Mike Quinsey

You may wonder at times what we do to fill in our time. Most of our duties are involved in studying data that is collected by our computers. For example, we constantly monitor sites where weaponry is ready to be used. Our brief is to ensure that those weapons of mass destruction are not used, to the point where if they are launched we will destroy them. We are also intent on preventing false wars, and any attempt to raise the tension between rival countries. We are holding back progress towards any further attempts to repeat a 9/11 scenario, because as you will know the Dark Ones create chaos and fear whenever they can. It is not just the Galactic Federation that are involved, but also our allies who are often placed at the heart of things. In general terms, we monitor Mother Earth, so that we able to predict where and when changes will occur. That gives us time to take action to limit the dangers, as we cannot interfere beyond the margins we are given. Mother Earth must be allowed to proceed with her ascension, and that is course vital if you are to go forward with her.

As we sometimes mention to you, our plans are continually being updated according to the feedback we get from our computers and earthly sources. We know where events are likely to proceed to but not necessarily in detail, as a number of options usually exist. The main point is that the outcome of this cycle is assured, and in no circumstances will that be altered. In due course you will all learn of what is planned, and it will give you back your freedom and prepare you for ascension. There are times when you feel that there is no defense against the Dark Ones, but since we know what they plan their threat is limited by us. Remember that we must respect the laws of freewill, and the karmic situations that you have been responsible for. These may go back eons of time, and can be played out at any time when it is appropriate. Your reason for going through duality is to learn lessons, and it would not help you if we shortened them.

If necessary we are on call throughout the whole Universe, and have millions of ships in our fleet at our disposal. There are also millions of personnel from the different civilizations that work with us, so in fact we can spread them far and wide. They are all like us inasmuch that they have achieved high levels of spirituality, and live in the higher dimensions that have moved well beyond duality as you know it. So why are we here you may ask, and the answer is that all ascended Beings act in service to other souls that are moving into the Light. Also, your whole Universe is involved in ascension and that is quite an important event. Because you need help to ascend, what is being given to you may be looked upon as disproportionate assistance according to your size. By other standards, even in your own solar system, you are in fact quite a small planet. However, your place in ascension is so vital to a successful completion, that a strong focus is placed upon the Earth and its inhabitants. This will ensure that regardless of what happens in the meantime, you will succeed in reaching your goals.

Our work is not organized in the same way that you are used to experiencing. We have no need to confine ourselves to strict times of working, although we take our responsibilities very seriously. It is our life, and a pleasure to serve others, and not in the least boring. We are happy at our work, and since we do not use money, we have no competition for jobs based on remuneration. All skills are employed where they can be used to our best advantage, and there are no square pegs in round holes. Work is not tiring as we do not experience fatigue because our bodies are more refined than yours, and we continually re-energize them from the energies around us. We can enjoy some small refreshments or light food, but that is more for pure enjoyment. In time you will also reach such levels. Your needs are different as you have a heavy physical body to support, and eating is both essential and a pleasure for you. However, you will find that as your new body develops and becomes more refined you will eat less.

As you are beginning to understand, the changes you are to experience will be far-reaching and a new Human will emerge. You will go from the illusory lower dimensions, to the levels of spirituality that respond only to the Light. All is in harmony and balance, unlike the imbalances you experience upon Earth. The contrast is so great that it is hard for you to imagine moving from hell to heaven, but that is how it will strike you. Perhaps the most impressive experience will be feeling the love energy that pervades the higher dimensions, where only the truth can exist.

Bearing in mind what you are learning about your future, we might comment on the need to keep focused on it, and do not allow earthly matters to distract you. What is of the old has served its purpose, and the new is waiting to be introduced. First must come the cleansing, and the restoration of your rightful entitlement to all that is given to you for your use by the Creator. By the time you reach the end of the cycle, you will already well along the path to ascension and ready to go even further. As is often emphasized, the end times are simply the end of duality, and life goes onto to the next stage. At present you are a poor reflection of what you are destined to be.

When you suffer your aches and pains your disappointments and fears, can you imagine being free from them, because that is your promise. Duality has been a hard lesson to go through at the levels you are in, but your progress up the spiritual ladder has been phenomenal. Nowhere else could you have achieved such results. Perhaps fortunately in some ways, you cannot remember your past lives and know how hard it has been to make progress. That is not important however, as it is what you take from them that determines how far and how quickly you evolve. Those of you who have awakened are able to attract the Light to you, and unless you have an exceptional lapse you are assured of ascending.

I am SaLuSa from Sirius, and like to give you acclaim where it is warranted. You are wonderful souls that stand at the door of release from all of the attachments to the lower dimension. They cannot in any event exist in the higher ones, and everything is being done to help you do so.

Thank you SaLuSa.

— Mike Quinsey

(The above message was given to Mike Quinsey on August 20, 2010)

" ... evolution doesn't occur in a vacuum. It feeds the expanding energy field, which has been called 'the source,' 'universal mind,' 'collective consciousness' and also the Akashic Records. Considered by physicists and philosophers as the vibrational dimension where all that's been thought, felt or done on Earth has been and is still being recorded, it is where all that happens to one Soul impacts every Soul." — Barbara Schiffman

2012 and Beyond Through the Eyes of the Akashic Records

by Barbara Schiffman

Quantum physics and metaphysics agree that everything is energy in the process of evolving — including humans, the Earth and even time.

But evolution doesn't occur in a vacuum. It feeds the expanding energy field, which has been called "the source," "universal mind," "collective consciousness" and also the Akashic Records. Considered by physicists and philosophers as the vibrational dimension where all that's been thought, felt or done on Earth has been and is still being recorded, it is where all that happens to one Soul impacts every Soul.

In Sanskrit, Akasha is defined as the "primary substance of Spirit." In the film *Defending Your Life* with Albert Brooks and Meryl Streep, the Akashic Records were depicted as movies Albert watched from his most recent life to help him evolve. The Records have also been accessed by psychics and seers like Edgar Cayce whose accurate trance-state medical and past-life readings began to popularize the Akashic Records in the 1930s and '40s.

Each individualized Akashic Record contains not only an energetic blueprint of the Soul of a person, place, animal or event but also "the story of (its) journey through time." This story "changes to reflect (its) growth in consciousness," according to Linda Howe, author of the best-selling books *How to Read the Akashic Records* and *Healing Through the Akashic Records*.

The Records do not reflect a "destiny" set in stone — they're fluid wavelengths evolving via the individual, group, regional and global activities which constantly reshape and redirect energy. Just as each Soul has its own unique Record – which Judeo-Christian religions call "The Book of Life" — so do dates and events, especially those with far-reaching impact like 1/1/2000 (aka Y2K) or 9/11/2001.

On 12/29/09, I tuned into the Akashic Records of the forthcoming year 2010 using Linda Howe's Pathway Prayer Process© as my vibrational access-key. The Akashic Records of 2009 told me it's time for each human on Earth to take responsibility for their personal vibrations as well as those of everyone and everything connected to them. "Learning this and accepting it and taking it seriously for the whole planet and human beings" was to be 2010's energetic focus. This played out as people came together to deal with the Gulf oil spills, earthquakes and tsunamis around the world, and escalating shifts in the traditional structures of commerce, religions and governments, among other events with global impact.

The Records also said it would be helpful to "let go of the old, be open to what's new and universal" and trust that what seems like chaos, "push/pull" and confusion is really part of the path to clarity. This message continues to be relevant.

For this book, I accessed the Records of 2012 and received these insights:

"The date 12/21/2012 is connected to the turning of the Mayan calendar as a means to focus the collective consciousness of humanity on the current requirements of evolution. It is not a date or day to be feared or revered. This is similar to how the events of 9/11/2001 centralized the attention of everyone on Earth for the common good.

"What is most critical to 2012, however, is already stirring within every human, animal, tree and rock: a quickening of the frequency that binds everything together and always will. Everything vibrates — the stars, Earth, air, oceans, people and even time. As the Akashic Records of 2012, we hold the collective vibrations of each one and all of these.

"Many things have been said, written and predicted about this time on Earth in relation to dates on man-made calendars and events that may not occur as what is to come is still evolving. The subtle and amplified frequency shifts occurring between today and the calendar-date related to the Mayan Calendar (12/21/12) will shape what occurs more strongly than any predictions made so far by human minds and egos.

"It is the collective energy of all humanity that influences how the Earth, sun and stars resonate with humans and with each other. People of the past were more aware of this as they were attuned to the subtle energies of the Earth, sun and stars. People today are increasingly desensitized due to the abundance of manufactured electronic energy which overlays the natural frequencies connecting each human to each other and the Earth.

"Creating a new equilibrium and maintaining balance between the natural world and the new, yet necessary, global connectivity via electronic pathways and airborne wavelengths is essential to prevent the Earth and humanity from imploding. This is more likely than the dire Hollywood predictions of explosions and disasters.

"But there is good reason not to wait until 2012 for humankind to take full responsibility for the impact of all thoughts, emotions, behavior and mental projections on everything on Earth as well as the cosmos beyond. Whether you believe mankind began elsewhere or will shift to other dimensions at some point does not change the fact that it is at an evolutionary juncture. There is a critical mass of humans on the planet using technologies that can unbalance Nature. So it is vital for humans to raise their own vibrations and harmonize these technologies with Nature while they are still in physical form.

"If this can be done before 12/21/12, an atmosphere of peace, calm and connectedness will infuse the Earth, sun and stars. This will help them align without releasing energy that could overwhelm human electronics and physical fields. Making time to consciously vibrate at the frequency of peace and unity will calm and connect each individual on Earth. By tuning into the collective energy of the Records and 'feeding' them with positive light and love, each of you will also receive more light and love directly and continually.

"This shift in vibration, consciousness and conditions will not occur in one 'big bang,' but it will be felt by those whose vibrations have been able to rise an octave or two, although things will seem the same in the outer world. This critical mass can bring everyone into a new alignment if it can be generated in time.

"If so, the transition from 2012 to 2013 and beyond will bring forth a new unity, seemingly for no reason. But good reasons will appear in abundance in 2013 as balance is restored. New discoveries in science, the medical field and technology will be equaled by an increased understanding of humankind as one species regardless of skin color, language, age or economics.

"Humans will begin living from the perspective of Soul rather than Body by realizing there is more to life than what is experienced in one lifetime. This will shift humanity's focus to treating the Earth as the mother of all tangible creation by making everyone 'seed planters' and nurturers for future generations.

"Humans will celebrate their unique differences and creativity rather than kill each other because of them. By accepting that the body each Soul is temporarily born into is merely a vehicle for the essence of Creation, everyone will begin to feel — and act — like a vital and ever-evolving part of All That Is. These connections will become more important than differences between humans as a new appreciation of life's holistic system will fuel the potential to further evolve."

(Barbara Schiffman is a Certified Akashic Records Consultant and Teacher who helps people live from their Soul's point of view through individual readings (in person and by phone), workshops and writings.
     www.YourLifeandSoul.com and Barbara@YourLifeandSoul.com)

Many Worlds, Many Destinations

by Adonna

My first vision of the future occurred in March of 1982. After a period of social and geophysical upheaval, I saw people dressed in white appear in various places around the world, and the people near them were reassured and calmed. Everyone in these groups were taken up onto the ships, and then a catastrophic shift occurred that left the planet a barren rock, as everything that was not bedrock had been flung off into space and did not return.

The ships took us to a spherical mothership approximately 80% of the size of the Earth, and several years passed. We were physically transformed into perfected bodies and experienced a change in our consciousness while the planet herself transformed, ascended and manifested as a totally new planet, in a different frequency band.

My vision moved forward in time and I experienced the new planet (Terra), now colonized. I heard the Music of the Spheres and I could see and feel that everything on the planet was radiant and expressing quiet joy. I saw Christ presiding over this new world, and he sent me back to my mundane experience with the words, "You will be called. In the meantime, be in a prayerful attitude, waiting."

"And I saw a new heaven and a new earth, for the first heaven and the first earth had passed away, and the sea was no more." Rev. 21:1

This is the passage that Dolores Cannon quoted in her chapter titled, "Planetary Transformation: The Coming New Earth," and it perfectly describes my vision as well.

In her other chapter, "Preparing for the New Earth," Dolores describes a vision that Annie Kirkwood had, showing the Earth dividing into two parts, like a cell dividing — the old Earth and the New Earth. Dolores reports that one of her clients has said, "The world which you envision is already inside of you. You are not moving to another planet. You are breaking out of your shell. This planet — this shell — is bringing forth that light."

I think both of us might be right in what we expect, except that I feel that this present world is going to give rise to more than just two alternative

209

realities, as I discuss below.

The next confirmation of what I had been shown came in 1985, when I discovered the book, *Project World Evacuation*, by Tuella. However, in Tuella's version, it seemed to me that she described a return to a repaired version of this planet, not a totally new one.

Others who have contributed articles that are included in this book, such as Sheldan Nidle, Mike Quinsey, and Hunt Henion, have come to the same conclusion. Their channeled messages and personal visions of what is coming, how these new possibilities will come to fruition, and how the changes that are needed will come about, somehow reflect a changed and upgraded version of our present planet, not the emergence of a totally new one.

Some, such as Steve Bhaerman, Martine Vallée, Patricia Webb, Tracy Latz and Marion Ross, C. Norman Shealy, Brie Liberty, Adele Ryan McDowell, Paul Von Ward, Camille Leon, Wendell Fitzgerald, Nina Meyerhof and Rhonda Smith have focused on the improvements and shifts needed within the present systems to bring about a better world for all. Drunvalo Melchizedek speaks about a shift in the power distribution within the planet herself that will cause many of the coming changes.

Others such as Justin Wilkinson, Elizabeth J. Foley, Adele Ryan McDowell, Linda Martella-Whitsett, Tracy Latz and Marion Ross, Barbara Joye, Hunt Henion, Barbara Schiffman and Camille Leon have indicated that the necessary changes will come from within us, through our own personal shift and efforts. Still, all of these authors also speak about an unfolding taking place on this present planet, in this density or dimension.

In reading through the various articles in this book, there seem to be at least two different ways of describing both our coming destinations and condition. The term *density* refers to the way matter is packed. It is not a location, but a *physical* condition. According to the Hosts of Heaven (the source of my *Operation Terra* material), at each succeeding density, spiritual mass increases and physical mass decreases.

Both Suzanne Ward and the Hosts refer to this planet as a third-density planet, which describes the packing of the particles that make up its material mass. Ward indicates that the planet will move up into fourth density before ultimately residing in its destination of fifth density, but does not say how long that process will take. The *Operation Terra* material focuses on Earth's attainment of fourth density existence — a level that would seem like Paradise to us — and does not look beyond that.

Sylvia Bucek also refers to our present planet as a third-density planet, and does not identify the density of the New Earth she experienced, but it is clear that regardless of whether it is a transformed version of the present planet or a totally new one, the New Earth will be a glorious garden, indeed!

Linda Backman refers to the density of our planetary laboratory and ascension as the movement from that density into a condition where we are primarily light, a process that will only begin in 2012, not be achieved by then. Hunt Henion also says something similar, placing the major earth changes around 2014 and the big shift in density sometime after that. These differences in expectations regarding timing reflect the presence of several different timelines that will emerge from this one shared reality (see below).

Dimension is a vector quality. It indicates relative *location*. Time is also a vector quality, indicating location. Time has three dimensions and places events within the three dimensions of space, which is why we refer to the space-time continuum.

Several authors, such as Suzanne Lie, Adolphina Shephard and others, indicate that we are moving to a higher dimension. Used in this way, a dimension is a plane of existence and slices the reality pie somewhat differently than it might if density were the only variable. Some of these authors feel we are moving to the fifth dimension; others don't specify its level, only that it is higher than the one we presently occupy, which they all refer to as the third dimension.

In her description of how the various Rays travel, Anritra Melchizedek refers to many different dimensions. Savizar and Silarra, the third team of walk-ins associated with Extraterrestrial Mission, described a system having 13 dimensions, which is also the number identified by George Kavassilas.

Some authors, such as Dawn Newton and Colin Whitby, describe a physical transformation as well as a transformation in the way things will be done. Barbara Schiffman's look into the Akashic Records for 2012 indicates the unfolding of a process, which is not so much a single event in time, but an ongoing process that, once it begins, will open up a whole new realm or further human development.

Anritra Melchizedek describes the energetic influence the various Rays will contribute to this process, and Adolphina Shephard emphasizes changing our frequency to ride with the Earth's change in vibration.

Amoraea Dreamseed speculates that we may be approaching a great leap of some kind and calls for us to engage our "Divine Blueprint." He says this is how we'll create an energetic pattern that will open doors for others to follow. This is something that the Hosts have said will be accomplished by the emergence of Terra in the fourth density as a totally positive-polarity planet, which will provide an energetic pathway that can be followed in a future incarnation by those remaining in third-density worlds at this time.

And since we live in a multidimensional, reciprocal universe, Hunt Henion and Rhonda Smith have given us a peek at the symbols underlying the shifts taking place now and their possible significance in recognizing the larger intelligence at work behind the scenes, in the "grand design" that encompasses it all.

In 1984, I read *The Right Use of Will*, which asserts that our present global population was of mixed lineage. The book explains that after the coming shift, we will all return to our "right place," and that's when I got my first inkling that there was more than one destination or future ahead for us.

Then I read other books and met certain people who, in my opinion, were totally credible. Yet from their accounts, it was clear to me that they were expecting to experience a very different future than the one I had been shown. During a vision quest he experienced, David Sunfellow reported seeing 12 paths splitting off, and the Bible referred to the "new city" having 12 gates, so I began to suspect that there were at least 12 *different* futures that would emerge from this one shared reality.

Parallel universes have already been described by Fred Alan Wolf, among others. I intuitively embraced a metaphor of "timelines" as being like several different moving sidewalks in a large airport terminal, all moving along side by side at the beginning, and then beginning to diverge from each other to the degree that they ultimately disappear from each other's view.

Chet Snow's book, *Mass Dreams of the Future*, presented the data of three different researchers who made use of hypnosis to take 2,500 people 150 and 300 years forward in time and asked them to describe what they saw. They described six different, mutually exclusive "futures," none of which was the one I had seen, but each of which had arisen from approximately 5% of the present population.

The experiment might have different results if it were performed today. However, at that time, one of those futures was essentially a rubble world, with scavengers combing for useful items with which to survive. Another was a more pastoral, pre-industrial existence. Another was based in space, and yet another was housed in underground cities because the surface of the planet was not habitable and could only be traversed in some kind of protective suit. One was a high-tech, high-touch extension of our present world, with a more spiritual understanding.

In her chapter about the 2012 shift, Cat Thompson says that "The singularity we are approaching in 2012 can be seen as a cluster of possible realities and timelines, all converging together," and offers some advice about choosing which timeline one ends up upon. Cynthia Sue Larson (of "Reality Shifters") also talks about how we can walk between worlds and shift our reality.

Over the years, I've also come to the conclusion that each person was tuning in to the particular future that they were personally going to experience. The many different accounts given by the authors who contributed to this book may be an expression of these many different destinations, being described by those who will experience them. The vision I resonate with the most, independent of the details of how and when we get there, is the one put forth by E. Dee Conrad, in her chapter, "The Road to Tomorrow":

"Over the next few years, the world economy and its political structures will be flipped upside down. There is a great revolution coming, but it is not the kind where people march in the streets (although that will occur). No, the revolution that is coming involves our perception of reality and who we really are. You might call it a "silent" revolution because the battle for discovery — enlightenment — will be waged inside, not outside, each of us. It will change society forever, but it will not bring discord or trauma. Instead, it will bring unity the likes of which humanity has never experienced. It will bring an end to bloodshed and violence. It will bring humanity back to its essence — its true self — and along with it a new age of existence for the universe as a whole.

"This change will bring us to a new level of existence, a level that has never before been seen on this planet. This change will alter our perception of time, space, matter and reality in an instant. One day we will be standing here wondering what all the fuss is about, and the next we will have transcended into a world beyond our current comprehension. We will find ourselves in a world where existence is not measured in temporary accomplishments or trophies, but in lasting and permanent grace with full understanding of evolution, existence, and the laws of nature and the universe. For the first time, we will see our role in the universe. We will understand why we are here, at this moment, and why everything has

happened as it has. We will see the connection between our life and that of our neighbor. We will see the instant link between our thoughts and our reality. We will understand why our thoughts matter and how our emotions shape the world around us. We will see with perfect clarity who we are and all that we can be — all that we were meant to be. We will experience our true magnificence."

All of these things — all of these different scenarios and timelines — are going forward in tandem for now. At some point, all of these timelines will separate out from each other and have a different experience. I already see signs of that taking place. My advice is to listen within, FEEL into whether something resonates with you as "truth," and trust your own intuition within each moment that arises.

Everyone will end up at the destination their Oversoul has created them to experience. Everything you need to complete your journey will come to you, one way or another. We are all expressions of the Creator, and there is ONLY the Creator-in-expression. There are no accidents; there are no mistakes, and there *is* a plan for our journey that is uniquely ours. Trust in that and be at peace with everything else.

(Adonna is the custodian of and spokesperson for the material related to Operation Terra. You can read all of the available material at no charge at www.operationterra.com; you can reach Adonna at adonna@operationterra.com. The material is also available for purchase as printed books, online or through your local bookseller, anywhere in the world.

This article is copyrighted and may be distributed intact if proper credit is given and the web site and e-mail address is included.)

NOTES